CROSSCURRENTS *Modern Critiques*

CROSSCURRENTS *Modern Critiques*
Harry T. Moore, *General Editor*

Alan Ostrom

THE POETIC WORLD OF

William Carlos Williams

WITH A PREFACE BY
Harry T. Moore

Carbondale and Edwardsville
SOUTHERN ILLINOIS UNIVERSITY PRESS
Feffer and Simons, Inc.
LONDON AND AMSTERDAM

For William Carlos Williams and my wife
THE IRRESISTIBLE OBJECT
AND THE IRREMOVABLE FORCE.

LIKE THAT altogether different kind of poet, Wallace
Stevens, William Carlos Williams was an American phenomenon. Stevens had a full career in business, as a life-
insurance-company executive in Hartford, and yet he
wrote some of the most remarkable of all American
poems. Williams, whose verse is hardly less remarkable,
was a full-time physician practicing in New Jersey. Now
his poetry is the subject of this intensive study by
Alan Ostrom of Brooklyn College.

William Carlos Williams knew Ezra Pound from the
time they were both students at the University of
Pennsylvania in the early years of this century. Pound
soon went abroad for an almost permanent residence in
in England and then on the Continent; Williams (partly
educated in Europe as a child) was content to revisit
Europe, but for the most part stayed at home after taking
his medical degree at Pennsylvania in 1906. Williams'
early verse was somewhat derivative, although he was
almost at once quite modern, with his friends the
imagists. In 1917, with the rather experimental Al Que
Quiere!, Williams showed that he was finding his own
way. From that time forth, in both poetry and prose, he
spoke with his own distinctive voice. And it was a distinctive American voice.

Williams was seeing America, American things, so
freshly that Ezra Pound, in a 1928 essay, suggested that
Williams was discovering his native country virtually
with the eyes of an outsider: "One might accuse him of
being, blessedly, the observant foreigner, perceiving

American vegetation and landscape quite directly, as
something put there for him to look at; and his contemplative habit extends, also blessedly, to the fauna."

Williams' countrymen, however, didn't respond to his
vision and his idiom. At least, as Mr. Ostrom points out
early in the present book, the critics paid little attention
to him. Pound and occasional reviewers in Poetry magazine spoke well of Williams. In 1936 Babette Deutsch
in This Modern Poetry helped establish an important
place for him. Then, as the sections of Williams' Paterson
began to come out (the first four of the five to be completed appeared between 1940 and 1951), recognition
slowly followed; New Directions, publisher of that long
poem, brought out the first book on Williams in 1951
(by Vivienne Koch). In his later life (he died in his
eightieth year in 1963, five years after the last fully
finished part of Paterson), Williams received various
literary prizes and several honorary degrees. And a good
deal more was written about him. The interest has con-
tinued. In 1966, Williams was the first author to be
featured on a National Educational Television series
broadcast from a hundred stations.

Williams will probably remain among the leading poets
of his time. In a letter to Kay Boyle in 1932, he spoke of
some of his contemporaries, and of a few of them rather
coolly. Pound was, not surprisingly, "one of the few
moderns worth reading" but Robinson Jeffers was the
victim of his own "poetic diction." Edwin Arlington
Robinson seemed "stiff English. I can't see a flicker."
Ivor Winters was "bogged in ideas." But "Wallace Stevens
has something more than his play with sequences of
sound. His line, under that, was sometimes fluid. Worth
reading again." Williams came to think even more highly
of Stevens, however, and he liked Marianne Moore and
others. In 1932 his verdict of Frost was: "The bucolic
simplicity of Robert Frost seems to me a halt." And
surely, in any ultimate scoring, Williams should prove to
have written as many enduring poems as Frost.

One of the chief characteristics of Williams' verse is its
concreteness, about which Mr. Ostrom has much to say
that is valuable. Another important element in Williams'
poetry is the short line. Occasionally he swung long lines,
as in "A Goodnight" and in parts of Paterson, but usually

he wrote with a terseness that sharpened his epigrams and intensified his figures of speech. The tone and idiom were often colloquial; Mr. Ostrom discusses Williams' "Americanness" in relation to language as well as to sense of place. With language, the poet had "to find a new metric, some new means of measuring not only the sense of his line but its sound. The old methods, he saw, were useless"; they were "measurements of a language his world did not speak, of an old-world English rather than of a new-world American." Also, these "were too closely associated with structures of the past." Williams was indeed vitally helping to create what Mr. Ostrom several times refers to as "the twentieth-century risorgimento."

He divides his book into four long chapters, each taking its name in order from Williams' definition of a poem. Mr. Ostrom's own start is with Williams' ideas about verse writing, about what constitutes poetry. And he stresses Williams' sense of things, almost as pronounced (one might observe) as that of the nouveau-roman writers in France of today, who follow in the wake of Francis Ponge, a poet of somewhat the same concreteness as Williams, though with many differences of vision and, of course, of idiom. As Mr. Ostrom says of Williams, "by insisting upon 'no ideas but in things' he has forced his readers (many of them poets themselves) to discard their assumptions about the world, assumptions, for the most part, that permit men to avoid having to look at things; he has forced them to examine the objects in his poems for what they are in themselves, not for what they represent."

Elsewhere in his book, Mr. Ostrom says that "the inevitable final result of a technique, like Williams', that attempts to construct poems out of pieces of actuality is that it works always toward compression. . . . If this leads, perhaps, to less subtlety in the expression of intellectual materials, it does certainly lead to a great energy being pent up in the poem." Here, as always, Mr. Ostrom backs up his statements, in this case by quoting two versions of Williams' poem, "The Locust Tree in Flower," with helpful comments on the differences. It may be noted that Mr. Ostrom throughout his book quotes important poems from Williams. This helps to make his volume an introduction to the poet as well as a sophisticated commentary on his verse.

And this thorough and expert evaluation of Williams'
poetry is precisely what we need now. Although Mr.
Ostrom is particularly good on the subject of technique,
he doesn't (as much of the foregoing indicates) limit
himself to this aspect of his subject. He never really takes
his attention away from Williams' "central moral concern,
his concern with the propriety of all things as they exist
naturally (which is after all perhaps the primary concern
of every poet). . . ." If we accept this, Mr. Ostrom
points out, we see that Williams' "poems must inevitably
be an attempt to show (teach) us the truth, to differentiate for us reality and illusion, things in their real order
and the way we understand them (which is to say, often,
misunderstand them) and order them rationally and artificially—that is, the actuality in which we move." All this
is good and true, constituting another of the many
valuable observations in this continuously rewarding book.

HARRY T. MOORE

Southern Illinois University
March 4, 1966

CONTENTS

UNTIL THE LAST few years of his life William Carlos Williams was almost entirely neglected by the literary critics. Not only the academic critics, but the "little magazine" critics, too, acted, for the most part, as if he did not exist. Some few made passing references to him, and even fewer took him seriously; none wrote of him as a major figure of their time. Only after *Paterson* had forced their attentions did they begin to read Williams with much sympathy or any attention to detail. But by then the older attitudes had had their effect, and Williams' poems had been grown over with so much literary moss that one was hard put to find the real poem behind the misconceptions: such catchwords as *antipoetic* and *free verse*, *regionalist* and *primitive* had become firmly attached to the poems.

The young poets had all the while been reading Williams' poems, of course, and they had not been listening to the catchwords. As a result, Williams' importance as an influence in modern poetry grew until he became, in the late fifties, perhaps the greatest single force in American poetry. And so over the last few years Williams has suddenly become popular, not only in the avant-garde circles but in the academic world, in college courses in American literature. Students find themselves attracted to his hopelessly human view of things, and teachers discover that the poems lend themselves marvelously to analysis and interpretation.

Unfortunately, the old misconceptions still persist. The trickle of critical writing about Williams has not broken with the past, except, perhaps, to attempt from time to time to show that Williams never really was so unconventional after all; and what *has* been written that has been perceptive has been scattered and all too infrequent. And so it is my purpose here to bring together Williams' various sorts of poems and to discuss them both as broadly and as narrowly as possible. Not nearly enough attention has been paid to Williams' theories, I think, so I have begun by assembling and inspecting his statements of esthetic. By the same token, however, one cannot help noticing how rarely the writer of criticism about Williams actually bothers to look at the poems; and I have therefore attempted to illustrate wherever possible with poems, in part or in whole. But lest the reader begin to feel after a while that I have created an anthology, I must warn him that even the apparently large number of poems quoted is a small fraction of the total output of perhaps the most prolific of modern poets.

At any rate, I have broken with the common view of Williams where I have thought it inaccurate, though not, I hope, merely for the sake of argument. Beginning with Williams' ideas about the nature of poetry and moving to the kinds of subjects and the kinds of things to be found in the poems, I have gone on to his poems' structures and their language—a sort of what, why, and how of the poems. Hence the use of the opening lines of *Paterson* for chapter titles; they are Williams' own statement about the act of making poems:

> To make a start,
> out of particulars
> and make them general, rolling
> up the sum, by defective means—

Looking at these lines, I have had to wonder at times whether one could say more about Williams than he has already told us.

Passages are quoted from William Carlos Williams' *The Collected Earlier Poems of William Carlos Williams*, (New Directions, 1951), *The Collected Later Poems of William Carlos Williams* (New Directions, 1950), *Selected Essays of William Carlos Williams* (Random House, 1954), *The Selected Letters of William Carlos Williams* (McDowell, Obolensky, 1957), and *Paterson* (New Directions, 1963) with the permission of Florence

H. Williams and New Directions. British rights are granted by MacGibbon and Kee. Passages from Ezra Pound's *ABC of Reading* (New Directions) and Vivienne Koch's *William Carlos Williams* (New Directions, 1950) are quoted with the permission of New Directions. Passages quoted from *Selected Essays* by T. S. Eliot (Harcourt, Brace and Company, 1932) and *The Letters of Ezra Pound: 1907–1941*, edited by D. D. Paige (Harcourt, Brace and Company, 1950) are quoted with the permission of Harcourt, Brace and World, Inc.

ALAN OSTROM

Brooklyn College of
The City University of New York
December, 1965

ALLEN DEBUS

THE POETIC WORLD OF
William Carlos Williams

1 TO MAKE A START, OUT OF PARTICULARS

FLOWERS, says the romantic young man, are the subject of William Carlos Williams' poems; familiar, ordinary things, says the critic. In fact, such is the strength of these general impressions that rarely does a third "subject" come to mind without a great deal of deliberation. And there is good reason for this phenomenon, despite the obviously unfair incompleteness of the two appraisals: Williams has insisted, in prose theory as in poetic practice, upon the necessity for drawing the poem's materials from the familiar world, and in so doing he has turned frequently to the world of nature, and of flowers especially, for his particulars. The objects in his poems that people remember best are therefore the trees, locusts in particular, with their sweet, delicate white flowers and their tenacity for life; the wild field flowers: daisy, Queen Anne's lace, violet, mullen—but flowers often just nameless, left to the imagination for color and shape; the animals and birds—especially the kinds found in and about cities; rivers and all that they bear or contain; the things that men make and use in ordinary life, but especially working, mechanical things: cars, tools (like the famous red wheelbarrow), boats (tugs, barges, ferries); and, finally, the small objects that we so rarely notice at all, often pieces and parts of larger things, like tin cans in a refuse heap, a bit of broken bottle catching the sunlight, old boards, all the discarded and unwanted things, the "useless" things.

The unfortunate part of this view of Williams is that it is deceptive and even belittling, for these are only the paraphernalia of his poetic world, not its center. The true focus of his attentions is men. Perhaps his readers have failed to notice this fundamental reference because, in contrast to his materials, it is not unusual—it does not set Williams apart in a category that can be labeled and consequently will make unnecessary the work of our determining his real uniqueness and his true values. But he is not a poet of nature any more than he is a poet of the mechanical or of any restrictive class of things; his poetic world is as diverse as the actual. Even as a matter of simple statistical fact, his most often used material is people. What is deceptive about this anthropocentric world is that, like the other physical materials of his poems, his people are the ones he sees in the everyday world about him: he has not sought out the rare, the exotic, in the human realm any more than he has in the nonhuman. Until *Paterson*, in fact, Williams did not attempt to create a character whose traits, exaggerated past the limits of their normal actual magnitude, would serve to make him an inescapably noticeable (and notable) creation like the artistically real, but actually unreal, J. Alfred Prufrock. To have done so would have been to divert his art from its intended function. And the character of N. F. Paterson is itself not that *sort* of exaggeration or magnification because it is not of that sort of fictional reality; it is one great, complex metaphor, one term of which is the modern Everyman Paterson (city and/or man) and the other a vast series of analogues extending in magnitude from the trivial to the deliberately obvious exaggeration past the bounds of normality—what Williams calls "marvels." There is, in short, a very definite esthetic basis for what Williams has done that causes him to be incompletely understood; and it is necessary, therefore, to investigate his concept of the nature of art—and in particular, poetry—before one can go on to an examination of what he writes about and how and why he writes about it. In a letter to Henry Wells, of Columbia University, written in 1950, expressive of his dissatisfaction at realizing that although he was sixty-six and "accepted" as a poet, his remarks *about* poetry were still not receiving serious attention, he wrote:

As to essay number two, the one concerning my own wild stabs into the ether—there too I think you fail sufficiently to take into consideration my role as a theorist. I think you need a word on that to pull your remarks together. For I think that only by an understanding of my "theory of the poem" will you be able to reconcile my patent failures with whatever I have done that seems worthwhile. [d286]

Underlying and informing all of Williams' work is his complex of ideas about the nature of art and art's relation to the well-being of both the individual and society. For in Williams' concept of the thing, art can have only one dedication: man. Art for Art's sake is for him an unintelligible statement, and art for the greater glory of God is unthinkable as all modes of formalized worship and religion are unthinkable; only for man's sake must art exist, but not merely as a testament to man's greatness or as diversion from the actual world. The spirit bearing it, its origin and its end, must be its intention for men's *use*. In his typically American way, Williams has worked against the American popular tradition that art is by definition useless—at best a luxury, at worst an escape from the pressures of actuality—and therefore separated from, and opposed to, the "practical" and the "useful." Rather, he makes of it the same demands that as a self-consciously pragmatic nation we would make of the "productive" disciplines: usefulness. Like his major contemporaries, he desires to establish the poem as a weapon in the daily battle. In 1944, for example, considering even World War II as only an intensification of the general everyday conflict, given first importance by the immediacy of its effects upon our lives, he showed how the equation of daily battle to fighting war could be made reversible. He wrote:

> The war is the first and only thing in the world today.
> The arts generally are not, nor is this writing a diversion from that for relief, a turning away. It is the war or part of it, merely a different sector of the field. [b3]

The daily battle is the struggle, he believes, to live well in this world, a constant campaign to maintain uniqueness within the over-all similarity, and each act, including World War II, is (or should be) a local skirmish in the general war.

Williams demands of the poem, therefore, not that it

create merely more physical comfort, like a new car or a better can opener; he requires that it be a means, *the* means, to human wholeness. For not only is the poem not a luxury, he contends, it is a necessity. It is indispensable and irreplaceable. If a man is to fulfill himself as a unique being, it is only through the agency of art that he can do so. Art—and specifically the poem—is the usable means by which men may most fully realize their potential human- ity: it is the means to self, a real identity, for men both as individuals and as members of the collective whole.

This basic tenet of art's helping men to live their lives is identical to the ideas of Pound, Eliot, and Stevens. Williams' statements of the idea are reiterations, for himself and for them, of the intellectual and artistic position of the times; yet for him, as for them, it was not a matter of proposing plans for action, as it might have been for many of the writers of the thirties. These four poets were not interested in the artistic technology of "social protest," but in the poem's capacity to facilitate the growth of the mind. Theirs was the attempt to give men the most useful knowledge of all, the understanding of the nature of things. Thus Williams can say, in answer to the possible assertion that art exists for its mere being: "But I insist, yes, that the purpose of art IS to be useful." [c179] For a man writes, Williams believes,

> . . . to represent exactly what he has to say CLEAN of the destroying, falsifying, besmutching agencies with which he is surrounded. Everything he does is an explanation. He is always trying his very best to refine his work until it is nothing else but "useful knowledge." I say everything, every minutest thing that is a part of a work of art is good only when it is useful and that any other explanation of the "work" would be less useful than the work itself. [c180]

This concept of the function of art sets up an obvious opposition between art and whatever other disciplines one thinks of as leading to the expansion of knowledge, and thereby to the "good life." But especially it opposes art to the products of the rational faculties, philosophy and science, and their practical handmaiden, government (that is, politics). In this respect of conceiving art and philosophy in axiomatic opposition, not only is Williams at the artistic center of the whole revolution of the mind begun in the early years of the century, but he is, like

Stevens, Pound, and Eliot, for all his (and their) damnation of the Romantics, a true product and example of the Romantic movement. The idea is in fact central to much of the social structure and social theory of our time, but with this difference: the general belief is that art and science, imagination and reason, are mutually exclusive and that the choice between them is the process of deciding which shall be the *only* way to *all* knowledge and which shall be rejected and given a place on the periphery of life as an escape from knowledge into unreality. The thought forms a sort of syllogism, finally, that says: all that is not scientific is false; art is by definition not scientific; therefore art is false. In the concept that Williams holds, the opposition is between the means and kinds of knowing; there is no question of excluding one from our mode of living. Williams wrote a letter to Kenneth Burke in 1933 in which he tried to clarify his position for his friend, who was becoming increasingly interested in philosophy.

> The examples are missing, tho present in my head as circus performers, net makers—anything but machines—possessors of knowledge in the flesh as opposed to a body of knowledge called science or philosophy. From knowledge possessed by a man springs poetry. From science springs the machine. But from a man partially informed, that is, not yet an artist, springs now science, a detached mass of pseudo-knowledge, now philosophy, frightened acts of half realization. Poetry, however, is the flower of action and presents a different kind of knowledge from that of S. and P. [d137]

The immediate end of art, as of philosophy (science), is thus knowledge; the two disciplines are but different means to it. Not only are they unlike in their methods and their products, however; they differ in their intents, their natures, the qualities of their beings. For in Williams' understanding of the matter, philosophy (science) is static and separates part from part, while art is kinetic and holds the parts together; he believes that the artist

> differs from the philosopher [scientist] in point of action. He is the whole man, not the breaker up but the compactor. He does not translate the sensuality of his materials into symbols but deals with them directly. By this he belongs to his world and time, sensually, realistically.

His work might and finally must be expanded—holds the power of expansion at any time—into new conceptions of government. It is not the passive "to be" but the active "I am." [c197]

Because it is the process of abstraction and generalization, philosophy (science) is useful, but by itself it cannot sustain life. The sustenance of life—not merely the physical *or* the intellectual *or* the social *or* any other partial, external "life," but the whole inner life and the physical as it is an expression of the inner life—that is the province of art. For in art's concreteness, Williams contends, resides its vital force: it makes its own fictional (and thus real) world, which sustains not only its own fictional life, but the lives of men in the world of actuality. Playing with the irony of his switch in terms, Williams remarks:

It is theoretical, as opposed to philosophy, most theoretical when it is most down on the ground, most sensual, most real. Picking out a flower or a bird in detail that becomes an abstract term of enlightenment. [c198]

The concrete flower or bird "in detail" is an abstract term in the most literal sense of having been taken, picked out, from the larger mass of things; in addition to its own existence as a unique entity, therefore, it assumes a representative existence as a member of the class in which Williams has visualized it and from which he has taken it. This is its "theoretical" quality that varies in proportion able outcropping of evidence that implies the hidden to its realness, its sensuality: it is the perceptible, examin- order of things, and the better we can know it as it *is*, the better we can infer the order. Thus Williams can say in explanation of the poet's selection of detail:

The compactness implies restriction but does not mean loss of parts; it means compact, restricted to essentials. Neither does it mean the extraction of a philosophic essence. The essence remains in the parts proper to life, in all their sensual reality. [c198]

In these ways Williams forms his evaluations of the opposed disciplines of the mind. Science and philosophy are dessicants: in translating the thing *as thing* into a thing as conceptual symbol ("essence") so that it may be apprehended by the rational faculties—and *only* by the rational faculties—they preserve, not the living world, but its dried husks. Art is the superior mode by virtue of its sensuality; it is the agency of both form and action, which is the form of life.

If the immediate end of art is "useful knowledge," then implied is a further end in the application of that knowledge. That is, if the knowledge is useful, in what way can it be used? The indication has already been made that poetry helps a man to live his life by supplying him with an understanding of the nature of the world, but Williams is even more specific than that. He believes that because the form of the information given is not merely generalized classification by similarity, but a structure that illuminates the singularity of each thing as it belongs in that overall pattern of similarity, the poem contains the materials for the regulation of life: "Poetry is a rival government always in opposition to its cruder replicas." [c180] For the poem is structurally an image of the world we live in; its order is a replica of the relationships of the "inner reality" of things shown in terms of the physical actuality of those things as they exist in a dynamic state. The government of poetry, in other words, is the proper ordering of the world.

> So that the artist is dealing with actualities not with dreams. But do not be deceived, there is no intention to depict the artist, the poet, as a popular leader in the Rousseauian sense. Rather he builds a structure of government using for this the materials of his verse. His objective is an order. It is through this structure that the artist's permanence and effectiveness are proven. [c213]

Even a dictum like Coleridge's that the primary aim of art is pleasure does not contradict all this. To have an effect upon men, art must before all else give pleasure, which Williams sees as deriving from art's "sensuality"; the poem satisfies, not only the mind, but the senses. Only when it does this can the poem be properly accepted by the imagination and carry with it its understanding and illumination of the world. But Williams would also say that this is pleasure only in its simplest form, this fulfillment of the desire for rhythmic sensation or even for immediacy and clarity of mental image. He would assert that the highest pleasure is the product of knowledge, of the satisfaction of the desire to learn that, like Aristotle, he believes exists in *everyone*. Thus as the poet-speaker in "Writer's Prologue to a Play in Verse," Williams addresses his imaginary audience (which is any man, every man) with a consideration of their unfulfilled need:

> And is all they can think
> of to amuse you, a ball game? Or
> skiing in Van Dieman's land in August
> —to amuse you! Do you not come here
> to escape that? For you are merely
> distracted, not relieved in the blood,
> deadened, deafened, stultified.
> But this! is new. Believe it, to be
> proved presently by your patience.
> Run through the public appearance
> of it, to come out—not stripped
> but, if you'll pardon me, something
> which in the mind you are and would
> be yet have always been, unrecognized,
> tragic and foolish, without a tongue.
> That's it. Yourself the thing
> you are, speechless—because there is
> no language for it, shockingly revealed. [b13]

As Williams sees him in the poem, the poet is the voice, not just of a few, but of all men, calling out for greater satisfaction. In this dual role of representative man and, to use Pound's term, antenna of the race, the poet explains that in the play "We are not here, you understand, / but in the mind, that circumstance / of which the speech is poetry." [b12] Given these conditions, that men need (and if they think about it at all, wish) not to be distracted from life, but relieved of the burden of not knowing themselves, and that the agent of this relief is poetry, Williams concludes:

> For pleasure! pleasure, not for
> cruelty but to make you laugh, until
> you cry like General Washington
> at the river. Seeing the travellers
> bathing there who had had their clothes
> stolen, how he laughed! And how
> you shall laugh to see yourselves
> all naked, on the stage. [b15]

In a letter to John Crowe Ransom some five years after the publication of this poem, Williams has a comment that could have been a critical note, appended like the notes to "The Waste Land": "The secret of all writing, all literature, is escape, true enough, but *not* in the Freudian sense. It is not, in other words, evasion. But it *is* escape—from the herd." [d272–73] This is the secret in Williams' theory, not only for the writer (who is the immediate concern of the remark), but for the audience as well.

The aim of poetry is thus in this sense the pleasure of knowledge, ultimately self-knowledge—not narcissism, but the understanding and acceptance of one's own real being: of one's generic similarities to all other men and, over and above this, of one's particular uniqueness. For Williams, the poet is concerned, finally, with showing men what is the only worthwhile subject of art: men, as they are, as they might be. He will make available his understanding of what is man's place in the world: what are a man's relationships to other men and what are his relationships to the other, nonhuman things. He will illuminate the dark areas of men's existence. And whatever in the poem does not deal with men directly, but presents the nonhuman—this will be an illumination of men too, for this is that physical, actual world, or part of it, in which they live.

What cannot be too much stressed, therefore, is Williams' insistence on the poem's "sensuality." It is not a simply intellectual power that makes the poem for him an indispensable condition of life; it is, as he has said, the poem's rootedness in the physical world of actuality. The phrase from *Paterson* that has become—to his detriment in its frequent misconception—the critical touchstone for his work is in one of its meanings the proper statement of this quality: "No ideas but in things." Williams does not mean that the poem must have no ideas; his intent is quite simply that it ought to have no ideas as pure, unattached intellect, outside the limits of what is expressible by the world of actuality within the poem. Precisely because ideas are important they must root and live in the objects or relations of objects in the poem, since, Williams says:

A life that is here and now is timeless. That is the universal I am seeking: to embody that in a work of art, a new world that is always "real."

All things otherwise grow old and rot. By long experience the only thing that remains unchanged and unchangeable is the work of art. It is because of the element of timelessness in it, its sensuality. The only world that exists is the world of the senses. The world of the artist. [c196]

Only in the ordered sensuality of the poem, then, can ideas be sustained—by the constant presentness of the poem's "things." From this world the ideas may become explicit statements, rising, as it were, as the poet's imagined continuations of the structure of actuality in the poem, or they may remain unstated, implicit in the poem's order. In *Paterson* this esthetic condition is itself a central idea for Williams to investigate (even as he practices it), as his characterizing axiom might indicate; and in many of the short (or shorter) poems it is a main, or the only, subject. It is a flat statement in "A Sort of a Song" and "The Poem," and a main concern of "Writer's Prologue to a Play in Verse"; it is an interesting implication in "The Dish of Fruit"; in "The Clouds" Williams addresses himself to it in great detail; and it exists as direct statement, the whole subject, in "To a Solitary Disciple." Nor is this more than a random list.

"To a Solitary Disciple" is a particularly helpful exposition of the idea because it puts the matter into the form of object lessons: not only does it talk *about* what sort of thing to use in a poem—and how to use such things—but the poem attempts to teach by doing.

> *Rather notice, mon cher,*
> *that the moon is*
> *tilted above*
> *the point of the steeple*
> *than that its color*
> *is shell-pink.*
>
> *Rather observe*
> *that it is early morning*
> *than that the sky*
> *is smooth*
> *as a turquoise.*
>
> *Rather grasp*
> *how the dark*
> *converging lines*
> *of the steeple*

meet at the pinnacle—
perceive how
its little ornament
tries to stop them—

See how it fails!
See how the converging lines
of the hexagonal spire
escape upward—
receding, dividing!
—sepals
that guard, and contain
the flower!

Observe
how motionless
the eaten moon
lies in the protecting lines.
It is true:
in the light colors
of morning

brown-stone and slate
shine orange and dark blue.

But observe
the oppressive weight
of the squat edifice!
Observe
the jasmine lightness
of the moon. [a167–68]

This is one of Williams' early poems, published as part of Williams' book *Al Que Quiere* in 1917, only three years after the appearance of the issue of *The Glebe* devoted to *Des Imagistes*. Yet it is in no sense either an imagist poem or a plea for imagism; its sole relation to imagism is in its insistence upon clarity of image and its own accomplishment of that clarity. Williams' advice is addressed to the problem of creating a poetic world of sufficient "sensual" actuality to remain always in its own here and now. He begins the poem, therefore, by making clear the foundation for all his practice: first seek out the thing itself in its uniqueness and present that. Don't talk about secondary or abstracted or commonly held qualities, although they may be more "impressive," until the poem has established what the things are and how they are ordered. Avoid the *conventional* metaphoric observations (here of color and texture) because, he implies, they are sterile; they tell us nothing we need know. Only the direct statement of whatness contains within its sensuality—in addition to all the associational implications we can possibly want—the indispensable purely denotative knowledge of the thing as thing: the denotative fixes the poem's world in the presentness of actuality. But even the *new* metaphor cannot fix the world; seeking the similarity of essences as its source of validity, it leaves the "world" at best only partially formed, qualities floating in an abstract sea. *Begin,* then, Williams advises, by establishing a structure of actual things, which is the only sort of world we can know fully as men bounded by the limits of our senses. Only then can the extensions and the understanding of the nature of our world come.

Two suggestions about such an understanding of the first part of the poem have been made: (1) that Williams' use of "rather" indicates a preference, levels of importance, not that one method should be followed and the other avoided; (2) that Williams' central point is that the poet should see the poem and the subject as a problem in abstract design. It seems to me that in the first, the normal difference in degree expressed by "rather" has become extended to the point of its becoming a difference in kind. Williams is, of course, not asserting that metaphor must *never* be employed in a poem, but that it cannot be the *basis* of the poem. In this poem, as in a majority of his poems, he uses metaphor, but only after he has begun to establish the existence of an order of things as things. In this sense, he is saying, "Do not—yet." The second point is well taken, but in reference to the second part of the poem rather than the first, and if "abstract" is omitted. There is no indication that Williams considers either the poem or the subject as an abstract structure—unless "abstract" is taken to mean what Williams calls "restricted to essentials," certain details selected from the heterogeneous mass by the imagination and made into an order. Certainly Williams is concerned predominantly with design—or order; it is only in the order assumed by the poem (as a replica of actuality) that he sees the artist's permanence. But his

admonition is that the poet must, absolutely *must*, seek
out the real order of real things. In a letter in 1934 to the
editor of A *Year Magazine*, Williams went so far as to
say:

> "Simply physical or external realism" has an important
> place in America still. We know far less, racially, than we
> should about our localities and ourselves. But it is quite
> true that the photographic camera will not help us. We
> can, though, if we are able to *see* general relationships in
> local setting, set them down with a view to penetration.
> [d146]

He italicized "see" because he wanted to emphasize the
imaginative act of seeing as opposed to the mere physical
fact of seeing what the camera is capable of "seeing." Ten
years later he proposed a more complex, more sophisticated esthetic. He wrote to Horace Gregory:

> If, as I believe and keep always before my eyes, if art is a
> transference—for psychic relief—from the actual to the
> formal, and if this can only be achieved by invention, by
> rediscovery, by reassertion by the intelligence and the
> emotions in any and every age—and if the grand aspect of
> this living drive is, when it occurs, a culture, then, I say,
> our chief occupation as artists, singly and jointly, should be
> the clarification of form, new alignments, in our own
> language and culture. [d226]

The reader of Williams must never forget that Williams
conceives of both the relationships of materials and the
structure of language in the poem as products and images
of their time and place.

Thus, he says in "To a Solitary Disciple," only after
some of the denotative constants have been fixed in the
poem can one see the order, the pattern, clarifying; then
one can see the conflict between the true nature of the
"ornament," its finality that limits the design of the
structure bearing it, and the nature of that structure,
which is to extend infinitely in lines of liberation and
protection. The restrictive *fact* of social convention,
represented by the ornament-sign, is in opposition to the
inclusiveness of the human spirit. The ornament fails to
limit the converging lines because the imagination finds in
them an order that it continues: this is the order of the
true nature of things. In it the relationship of the human

to the natural is also manifest, expressible now both by the poetic structure and by metaphor. Thus, finally, after demonstrating in the distortion of colors by the morning light how there can be a discrepancy between the real nature of a thing and our perception of it, Williams can end with a juxtaposition of images in which he can be sure his ideas will inhere. He is sure that the actuality of the poem's world will validate his judgments, which are, after all, judgments in terms of that world. The things—the edifice and the moon: the human and the natural—have been established; so have their relationship and their implications. And the ideas live in them and in their order. At last Williams can use the implications of lightness and jasmineness as contradistinct from the implications of heaviness and squatness; the qualities are not, cannot be, separated from the specific, concrete objects in which they exist.

This poem serves also as an exhibition of two other fundamental concepts of Williams' esthetic: (1) the distinctions between reality, actuality, and ideality; and (2) the role of the imagination in the creative process. These two are for him closely related matters, and in order to understand fully his concept of what the imagination is and does (about which he has written a great deal), it is necessary first to see how he classifies existence (about which classification he has written very little). Though he does not name them systematically or even consistently, and the terms I use must therefore be my own, for Williams there are three modes of being: (1) that which we perceive with the senses (actuality), (2) that which *is* but may be unperceived (reality), and (3) that which we wish (ideality). Some such simple classification undoubtedly underlies the work of all good poets, as it underlies in a shadowy, half-realized way the life and thought of all thinking men. But for Williams, although he rarely writes about it explicitly, the separation and understanding of the various modes is important not only as a presupposed intellectual foundation for his work; it is important as subject matter, an unavoidable aspect of the confusion he sees in his world, and it is valuable as compositional method, a means of approaching phases of life that he feels cannot be dealt with satisfactorily by other, more direct, more conventional means.

The differentiation of reality from actuality is the most difficult to make, since one is always involved in the processes of everyday experience; but for this very reason it is also the most important to the reader as a source of useful knowledge in the poem. That is to say, it is Williams' contention that the world as we know it is often a distortion of the world as it exists objectively, independent of our understanding of it: not only is the extent of our knowledge at best incomplete, but within that partial body are illusions that we mistake for truth. For instance, if we consider normal daylight as the perfect illumination, the "brown-stone and slate" in "To a Solitary Disciple" are the reality of the undefined material in respect to color; but in the light of morning we "know" that the colors are "orange and dark blue." In a similar way we may consider the steeple as a merely physical object topped by the final ornament, or we may look past our conventional attitudes and consider the steeple as an expression of the human spirit that the ornament tries, but fails, to limit. Here, Williams would say, the senses report the physical fact accurately, but our knowledge is colored by our attitudes and opinions, which condition our understanding.

The world in which we live and on which we base our actions is for Williams, therefore, essentially the world of actuality, a world both physical and ideational; it is a place, that is, ordered by our beliefs about it. As such, dependent as we are upon our imperfect senses and fallible understanding, what we know as actuality *may* be identical with reality, but far more often than not the two differ, often to the point of diametrical opposition. Our limitations of the senses and, perhaps even more important, of the mind cause us frequently to accept the illusion of what we think is for the reality of what *is*. But if we are to live well in this world, Williams believes, we must found our actions, our lives, on the stability of truth, not on misunderstanding—on the useful knowledge of the nature of things rather than on the illusory surface of actuality. This, I think, is why Williams insists so much uniqueness of each thing, its true whatness: only by so doing can the poet show the *real* order of his materials, as distinct from the apparent order involving qualities ines- upon the duty of the poet being first of all to show the sential and very possibly extrinsic to the materials. In an introduction to the catalogue for a retrospective show in 1939 of works by his old friend the painter Charles Sheeler, Williams comments:

> I think Sheeler is particularly valuable because of the bewildering directness of his vision, without blur, through the fantastic overlay with which our lives are so vastly concerned, "the real," as we say, contrasted with the artist's "fabrications."
>
> This is the traditional thin soup and cold room of the artist, to inhabit some chance "reality" whose every dish and spoon he knows as he knows the language that was taught him as child. Meanwhile, a citizen of the arts, he must keep his eye without fault upon those things he values, to which officials constantly refuse to give the proper names.
>
> The difficulty is to know the valuable from the impost and to paint that only. The rest of us live in confusion between these things, isolated from each other by the effects of it, a primitive and complex world without air conditioning. It is the measurable disproportion between what a man sees and knows that gives the artist his opportunity. He is the watcher and surveyor of that world where the past is always occurring contemporaneously and the present always dead needing a miracle of resuscitation to revive it. [c231–32]

In Williams' view, then, not only may the discrepancy between actuality and reality be great, but it is constantly deceiving us and constantly being glossed over by the official means of "knowledge." It is therefore dangerous, he asserts, for we form our scales of values, we ground our ideas, we judge and guide our actions, in the mistaken notion that the two are the same. Our constant attempts to attain a more nearly ideal world go awry because we misunderstand both what exists and what we must do, what order we can and must give our world, if we are to achieve better lives. For ideality differs from both reality and actuality in one significant way: it is what we wish a thing to be irrespective of what the thing is, and as such, the ideal is totally dependent upon our attitudes, our understanding of what we see. It has no constant *direct* relationship to either reality or actuality, but the form of its desires is determined by our beliefs about the nature of the world we live in. If those beliefs are inaccurate, our wishes and the actions that spring from them will be perverted.

However, the only way to reach reality, he believes, is *through* actuality: "no ideas but in things" is the credo of a poet who knows that we do indeed live in a place where we must deal with what is about us. The world of theory, of hypothesis and idealization, has, and can have, no existence of its own, apart from what we bump into every day. Reality is expressible only in the things, the actuality, of our world. As Williams indicated in his letter to Ransom, poetry is an escape not from the world, but from illusion; unlike Wallace Stevens, who would escape from actuality's pressure by the counter pressure of the poem's ideal order, its differentness from actuality, Williams sees the poem's value in its ability to *use* the actual as its materials and give to them an order by (and in) which the reader can perceive the underlying reality. If the world is too much with us, we cannot help ourselves by fleeing it, but only by wrestling with it and coming to some sort of terms with it. The mind cannot go on forever in chaos, but it cannot remain sane in the flight to an ideal unreality. If the mind is to be refreshed and renewed, as it must in order that it live sanely in the world, it must periodically be given a glimpse of a fundamental order, a structure of reality; and the poem is the physical concretion of that order, the piece by which we may know (which is to say, imagine) the whole. The poem's true gift is the gift of sanity.

It is for all these reasons that Williams seeks constantly for those infrequent images of the poet's perception which can show actuality and reality in congruence, when to show one is to permit the reader's imagination to perceive a positive image of the other. When Williams cannot achieve this moment of revelation, or when he sees greater poetic virtues in a negative image, he inverts the process and presents an image of the actuality and its discernible *un*reality, leaving the reader to his own imaginative devices for determining what the reality is. Thus, in the first two stanzas of "To a Solitary Disciple" he adjures his friend to choose the observations of whatness that lead one to reality, rather than those statements of similarity that present inessential aspects of actuality. In the third and fourth stanzas Williams goes beyond the simple

notice of physical actuality to a more direct statement of
the reality of the relationships of steeple and ornament
and some of the implications that arise from their order.
He returns in the following stanza to a juxtaposition of,
first, an image of congruence of the two modes, the "eaten
moon" lying in "the protecting lines," and, second, an
image of their difference, the true colors of the slate and
the stone being distorted by "the light colors / of morning." Finally, Williams is able to oppose the essential
realities of the two representative objects, the "oppressive
weight" of the edifice, symbolizing restrictive social organization, and the "jasmine lightness" of the moon. This is a
juxtaposition and contrast that, in the light of our usual
concepts of humanity and its agencies of regulation
(whether secular or spiritual), certainly implies a sad
disjuncture between what is and what we believe (because
we wish it to be so).

Just as Williams gives a detailed example in "To a
Solitary Disciple," in the poem for which he is probably
best known, "The Red Wheelbarrow" (though it is really
only a section of the long poem "Spring and All"), he
gives merely the briefest possible account of his data;
except for one word at the outset that indicates his intent,
he leaves the actual world intact for the reader's interpretation.

> so much depends
> upon
>
> a red wheel
> barrow
>
> glazed with rain
> water
>
> beside the white
> chickens. [a277]

Here, as so often in his poems, the excitement and vision
of reality derive from Williams' using as the typical object
central to his order an object that the reader would not
have thought representative of the qualities that Williams
finds in it. This disparity between the conventionally
assigned values (actuality) and those newly discovered as
reality performs the same function as the bringing to-

I've always thought that a good poet
should be able to write a poem about
mathballs + get away with it.

gether of apparently unrelated things in conventional metaphor: it provides a fresh view of reality in the perception of the previously unseen relationship. There is an important difference, however, between Williams' method and metaphor; the individual metaphor is restricted to two elements (A is B), greater complexity coming only with extreme difficulty and loss of immediacy (A that is X is B that is Y), while this method of Williams' can accommodate a theoretically unlimited number of materials (some of which can themselves be metaphor, as they are in many of Williams' poems).

This brief poem is a good example of how, more than anyone else in modern American poetry, Williams has brought attention to the things of our world. By insisting upon "no ideas but in things" he has forced his readers (many of them poets themselves) to discard their assumptions about the world, assumptions, for the most part, that permit men to avoid having to *look* at things; he has forced them to examine the objects in his poems for what they are in themselves, not for what they represent. In this respect Williams differs considerably from Eliot. In his statement about the "objective correlative," Eliot said:

> The only way of expressing emotion in the form of art is by finding an "objective correlative"; in other words, a set of objects, a situation, a chain of events which shall be the formula of that *particular* emotion; such that when the external facts, which must terminate in sensory experience, are given, the emotion is immediately evoked.[1]

Obviously, this is a demand for a form of symbolism; Eliot is not concerned about *what* actuality is given so long as *some* actuality is given. What is important is the emotion (or, I presume, in some cases the idea) that the physical objects or actions refer to. But unlike Eliot's symbolic peach (or hotels, oystershells, fog, and so forth) in "The Love Song of J. Alfred Prufrock," Williams' red wheelbarrow, rain, and white chickens are there because they actually *are* there in our everyday world, our experience. That as typical objects they contain implicit extensions of meaning is certain; but these extensions inhere in the realities of the things themselves and in their place in our experience. On the other hand, Prufrock being what he is, the object of his digestive deliberations might equally have been anything from an apple to a water-melon: the thing *as thing* is not important. Nor is it a question of all words (and nouns in particular) being symbolic, or of Eliot's world being anthropocentric while Williams' world is not. It is true, of course, that a noun is not the thing itself but merely stands for it, but what is in question is not the word but the physical object, which itself is being used to represent something that is not a necessary, unique quality of the object's nature; and while Williams does not present people explicitly, the *implicit* center of his world (implied, to begin with, by the wheelbarrow's having been made and the chickens' do-mestication and consequent association with men) can only be man. Were the wheelbarrow a tricycle or an automobile, therefore, the "meaning" of the poem would be entirely different. The order caught in the poem, of the whole world suddenly centered about these objects, would be different; it might be equally true and equally useful, but, focusing as it would upon other objects and their different intrinsic qualities, it would not give us the *same* information about the real nature of the world.

The fact is that Williams is determined to make his poetic world a replica of the actual because the poem must be "useful." In this respect, it seems, his intent has always been mythopeic: by creating a replica of the actual world, at last by heightened sensitivity to it to pierce through actuality to the universal men and actions and qualities of mind that are at once unique and typical—the representation of reality.[2] Clearly this is his intent in *Paterson:*

> *To make a start,*
> *out of particulars*
> *and make them general, rolling*
> *up the sum, by defective means*—[e11]

and

> *in distinctive terms; by multiplication a*
> *reduction to one; . . .* [e10]

In so doing, the poem not only exists as a "living" entity by virtue of its "sensuality," but it serves as an object lesson, as information purified and, as he says, "CLEAN of the destroying, falsifying, besmutching agencies" [c180] that pervert our lives. The fullest articulation of this myth-making intent is, of course, in *Paterson*, where the figure of Sam Patch, for instance, is transformed from a merely odd historical character into a paradigm of human action. Williams creates (reveals) Patch's typicalness by placing him, in action, in an imaginative order of actions where by juxtapositions and associations Patch ultimately takes on the human associations of Mrs. Cumming, who fell over the falls and also became identified with them, and, in fact, of all the human or ideational qualities directly connected or associated with the falls. In his individuality he is their representative. In this poem also, the basic idea of the man-city Paterson is, in his various aspects, an attempt at a universal reality within a surface of unique reality. But, in fact, Williams' mythopeic intent does not exist only in *Paterson* or only in his long poems; it underlies virtually *all* his poems, short or long, as a fundamental esthetic condition of Williams' mind as he makes a poem.

The means to this mythopeic end is naturally the imagination. Like all good poets, Williams considers the imagination the motive force in art: it is the faculty that enables a man finally to distinguish reality from illusion, to establish in the poem orders that reflect and reproduce the true orders of the world. In one of the prose sections of serious intent in "Spring and All" (before it was reprinted in the collected poems with the prose removed and the sections titled instead of just numbered), Williams says:

> And if when I pompously announce that I am addressed —to the imagination—you believe that I thus divorce myself from life and so defeat my own end, I reply: To refine, to clarify, to intensify that eternal moment in which we alone live there is but a single force—the imagination.[3]

The imagination is, in this view, the sole way to living one's life well, and art is its expression; the purely rational will not do because it is by nature defective and limited. As early as 1920 Williams gave voice to his conviction (which he had had, obviously, for some years) in the prologue to *Kora in Hell* defending its improvisations:

> The imagination goes from one thing to another. Given many things of nearly totally divergent natures but possess-

ing one-thousandth part of a quality in common, provided that be new, distinguished, these things belong in an imaginative category and not in a gross natural array. To me this is the gist of the whole matter. It is easy to fall under the spell of a certain mode, especially if it be remote of origin, leaving thus certain of its members essential to a reconstruction of its significance permanently lost in an impenetrable mist of time. But the thing that stands eternally in the way of really good writing is always one: the virtual impossibility of lifting to the imagination those things which lie under the direct scrutiny of the senses, close to the nose. It is this difficulty that sets a value upon all works of art and makes them a necessity. The senses witnessing what is immediately before them in detail see a finality which they cling to in despair, not knowing which way to turn. Thus the so-called natural or scientific array becomes fixed, the walking devil of modern life. He who even nicks the solidity of this apparition does a piece of work superior to that of Hercules when he cleaned the Augean stables. [c11–12]

Against this petrifaction of the mind is directed the "inventive imagination." The word "inventive" is important because it represents for Williams the use of the imagination in the creation of the poem; it indicates that the imagination is not only active, but productive of structures in an imitation of nature. Over and over he has spoken of the poet as inventing, and for him this is a specific process in which there are specific agents and specific goals. In the first place, the imagination is the informing force, but not to the exclusion of conscious reason; Williams wrote in 1942 to Harvey Breit that

It's all right to give the subconscious play but not *carte blanche* to spill everything that comes out of it. We let it go to see what it will turn up, but everything it turns up isn't equally valuable and significant. That's why we have developed a conscious brain. [d194]

From the marriage of the productive, primarily subconscious imagination and the directing, conscious reason comes the invention, an act in imitation of the processes of nature. Williams emphatically refuses the concept of art as a *copy* of nature:

It is NOT to hold the mirror up to nature that the artist performs his work. It is to make, out of the imagination, something not at all a copy of nature, but something quite different, a new thing, unlike any thing else in nature, a thing advanced and apart from it.

To imitate nature involves the verb to do. To copy is merely to reflect something already there, inertly . . . But by imitation we enlarge nature itself, we become nature or we discover in ourselves nature's active part.[4]

Invention is, in fine, the act of making concrete in the poem what the imagination has ordered in the mind. He says in "A Sort of a Song":

> —*through metaphor to reconcile*
> *the people and the stones.*
> *Compose. (No ideas*
> *but in things) Invent!*
> *Saxifrage is my flower that splits*
> *the rocks. [b7]*

Metaphor is a product of the imagination and can be understood only by that faculty; "saxifrage" (which literally means "rock-breaker") is by implication the creative imagination, which in the process of invention, of making the poem, breaks up the petrified assumed orders of actuality and creates new orders in the poem more consonant with the reality of their component parts. This is the poem's indispensability.

> *Without invention nothing is well spaced,*
> *unless the mind change, unless*
> *the stars are new measured, according*
> *to their relative positions, the*
> *line will not change, the necessity*
> *will not matriculate: unless there is*
> *a new mind there cannot be a new*
> *line, the old will go on*
> *repeating itself with recurring*
> *deadliness: without invention*
> *nothing lies under the witch-hazel*
> *bush, the alder does not grow from among*
> *the hummocks margining the all*
> *but spent channel of the old swale,*
> *the small foot-prints*
> *of the mice under the overhanging*
> *tufts of the bunch-grass will not*
> *appear: without invention the line*
> *will never again take on its ancient*
> *divisions when the word, a supple word,*
> *lived in it, crumbled now to chalk. [e65]*

Thus, in making his imagination the informing life of the poem Williams forces the reader to use his own. This is a matter that causes the unimaginative reader to put down Williams' poems saying that they are shallow or pointless—or worse. For Williams has little use for the purely logical or the merely "profound" *thought*, in or out of the poem; for the honest crackle of "the active 'I am'" of the image, it substitutes the meretricious boom of the empty "passive 'to be.'" Take, for example, not only *what* he says in the poem "Aigeltinger," but his way of presenting the images of the actual world in its simplicity of overt action and complexity of unknown processes and relationships of cause to effect—all this juxtaposed with the triviality of both what Aigeltinger does and the terms in which he is presented.

> *In the bare trees old husks make new designs*
> *Love moves the crows before the dawn*
> *The cherry-sun ushers in the new phase*
>
> *The radiant mind*
> *addressed by tufts of flocking pear blossoms*
> *proposes new profundities to the soul*
>
> *Deftness stirs in the cells*
> *of Aigeltinger's brain which flares*
> *like ribbons round an electric fan*
>
> *This is impressive, he will soon proclaim*
> *God!*
>
> *And round and round, the winds*
> *and underfoot, the grass*
> *the rose-cane leaves and blackberries*
> *and Jim will read the encyclopedia to his*
> *new bride—gradually*
>
> *Aigeltinger you have stuck in my conk*
> *illuminating, for nearly half a century I*
> *could never beat you at your specialty*
>
> *Nothing has ever beaten a mathematician*
> *but yeast*
>
> *The cloudless sky takes the sun in its periphery*
> *and slides its disc across the blue*

They say I'm not profound
but where is profundity, Aigeltinger
mathematical genius
dragged drunk from some cheap bar to serve
their petty purposes?

Aigeltinger, you were profound [b65–66]

The basic ironies here are clear enough. The poet (perhaps Williams, especially because of the supposedly "unpoetic" materials in his poems) is thought shallow because instead of using abstract symbols he offers images of actual things; because it is a replica of the natural world and thereby apprehensible, his product is not "impressive." Yet it is that very quality of physical reality that makes impossible the poem's perversion to selfish personal purposes. In contrast, people call the mathematician profound because of the impressive difficulty in comprehending his arbitrarily chosen symbols—and despite (or is it because of?) the obvious perversion of his intent and his services. As the process of the rational faculty, therefore, "profundity" consists of breaking down the physical, of defeating the senses, of substituting the abstraction of "God!" for the actuality of life as it is lived (the image in the following stanza). And in its conventionality as the "meaning" of the physical world of the previous stanzas, what a marvelously insipid proclamation it is!

Williams' method is very simple. He establishes the imaginative array in the first stanza, each image of "beginning" having something in common not only with the others in that stanza's individual order, but with the beginnings (or awakenings) that follow. Comparison of the natural (imaginative) with the rational placed side by side turns up only disappointment, however, as the richness of the poet's world of things degenerates into abstract thought: "The radiant mind" cheapens to the "deftness" stirring in Aigeltinger's brain; the "tufts of flocking pear blossoms" are mocked by the image of flaring "ribbons round an electric fan"; even the brain itself becomes, implicitly, a machine turning round and round. And it is this degeneration that will "proclaim / God!" It is the mathematician, who cannot be beaten at his specialty by anything—but yeast, the lowest form of life, no mathematician ever having been able to determine the formula for yeast's process of growth; yet the whole poem is concerned with beginning, reproduction, growth: the trees about to leaf, the mating crows, the dawn, the pear blossoms not only promising fruit but fertilizing the mind, the new bride and Jim making their knowledge grow by reading about the actual world. It is, finally, the scientific mind drunk and subservient to "their petty purposes" that is "profound." But the world continues to consist of the winds, the grass, the rose-cane leaves, the blackberries, the flocking pear blossoms, sun, dawn, sky, seasons, and the people who can know them only as things, by the senses, for whom they must be ordered, can only be ordered, lifted out of the distortions of conventional thought, by the imagination.

It is in the light of these basic esthetic conditions that one must see the materials of Williams' poems if one is to understand what the poems are about. I say, "what they *are about*," not "what they *mean*," which is something else entirely and quite outside the bounds of my intent—first, because "meaning" is a subjective thing dependent upon all sorts of matters ranging from the nature of the reader's physical, emotional, and intellectual experience to the state of his mind at the moment of reading and, second, because a poem's "meaning" is as much contained in its sound and in its structure, in its physical being, as in its "content." Or as Pound says in *ABC of Reading*:

> The term "meaning" cannot be restricted to strictly intellectual or "coldly intellectual" significance. The how much you mean it, the how you feel about meaning it, can all be "put into language." [5]

For example, as regards the poem "Raleigh Was Right," one could say immediately that it is concerned with the relationship of the individual man (or men) to the natural world, of man to the social world, and of the present to the past. But its meaning is surely nothing simple, like: "The development of our socio-economic system has destroyed our sense of unity with (and appreciative understanding of) the world of nature, which we *seem* to have had (but probably didn't) in the past." Nor is it anything of like kind, only more detailed and more complicated. The poem *is* what it means: everything from Marlowe's "The Passionate Shepherd to His Love," idealizing the country in the pastoral convention, to Raleigh's "Reply" by the "realistic" maiden who looks past the summer ecstasy of love and flowers to the time when "The flowers do fade, and wanton fields / To wayward winter reckoning yields," and the country (and all else physical, even as love itself) is no longer ideal; everything from the combination of these two to Williams' strictly modern approach to them and their dispute; from the poem's over-all structure to the length of the individual lines, to the sounds of the words—all this and more enters into the general meaning that readers might accept as the common denominator that they could then make personal. To attempt any discussion of "meanings" would thus be a pointless effort here; such an attempt is the proper burden of an entirely different sort of work in which a few poems can be considered in great detail and from varying points of view. What *can* be done, however, is to determine what are the typical subjects of a number of Williams' poems, and what are the materials, the things, of which he makes his poems' world.

It is wise in discussing any poet's work to make a differentiation between the subjects and the materials, the things he *uses*; but in Williams' case to do so is an absolute necessity, for in his seeking to find new material *anywhere* in his world, he frequently departs so far from the conventional "poetic" objects and their conventional references and associations as to confuse or even mislead the conventionally trained reader. The confusion does not stem from Williams' having imposed private, arbitrary symbolic values upon things, as Eliot has often done; it is a result of his imaginative ordering of those "things of nearly totally divergent natures but possessing one-thousandth part of a quality in common" that Williams searches out as the things in which his ideas shall reside. Given his contention "no ideas but in things," that is, and his equally strong conviction that the poem must break the reader's mind out of conventional (useless) patterns by creating new orders, it is evident that the "differentness" of his poems' actual world and the seeming unrelatedness of its various objects would cause many readers either to mistake what he *uses* for what the poem is *about* or even at times to fail completely to comprehend what happens at the surface level of actuality. In short, one must be careful to remember that the things are *not* ends in themselves; they are the representatives, in wholes of greater or less complexity, of the conceptual subject or subjects.

In her book *William Carlos Williams*, Vivienne Koch fails constantly to make this subject-materials distinction, just as so many other critics have done. At one point, she criticizes Kenneth Burke for having said of Williams' theory of art that "The process is simply this: There is the eye, and there is the thing upon which the eye alights; while the relationship existing between the two is a poem," [6] and "His hatred of the idea in art is consequently pronounced, and very rightly brings in its train a complete disinterest in form." [7] Having offered her objection, however, Miss Koch reveals to us that what bothers her is not the implication that Williams is uninterested in, even incapable of, ideas, but that "Burke has foundered on a spurious identification of form and idea. To reject 'ideas,' if this is Williams' heresy, is not to reject form, order, in the creative act." [8] Nowhere in her book, in fact, does she try to extirpate this concept of Williams as anti-idea. Yet until the publication of *Paterson* it was the generally accepted belief; and even now, I suspect, critical opinion pictures him as uninterested in ideas *except* in *Paterson*.

Bemused by his unusual (because for the most part homely and not "poetic") materials, readers have thus made two incorrect assumptions: first, that things are his total concern, and, second, that because those objects and their relationships are new to us, because the things typify and represent classes in which we do not ordinarily place them, Williams writes about matters different from both his contemporaries' and his predecessors'. Actually, both impressions are parts of the same error. In the first place, it is obvious that at the level of subject the conceptual fully enters Williams' work. For instance, as we have seen, "The Red Wheelbarrow" is not a mere descriptive list of things that Williams has seen somewhere: to say that he writes *about* wheelbarrows and chickens would be to ignore the words "so much depends / upon." These imply that the objects used exist in a necessary relationship to each other and to the rest of the world; a change in them would cause a change in the whole order of existence and in the viewer's life. But the statement also implies that we do not consider these specific objects or the whole class of ordinary "prosaic" things that they typify as we should; it is Williams' contention that we merely accept them as there—without curiosity, without thought, without really *seeing* them. Williams' idea, inherent in his poems' physical construction, is like the hidden part of the proverbial iceberg, unseen from the surface, but many times larger than what we see, and it is this idea about the nature of the world and men's attitude toward it that is the real *subject* of the poem. As another example, the primary subject of the previously quoted "To a Solitary Disciple" is the art of poetry, but there is no overt mention in the poem of poetry, writing, words—or esthetic theory. Were it not for the title, the reader would have no immediate direction toward the true conceptual subject, what the poem is about.

The subjects of poetry are a finite number of general ideas that are concerned always with the same matters; what change are the individual poets' personal emphases and the materials that they choose for their representations. These differ with the times, with the poets' cultural environments, and with the poets' inherent personalities. Thus it is that the wild, free, often drunken Dylan Thomas refused to use a pub (or bar) as an object in a poem because, as he announced once at a poetry reading, "It isn't 'poetic.'" But the genteel Mr. Eliot will use it, and gladly! [9] And thus, too, the subjects in Williams' poems are conventional enough individually, but unconventional as imaginative orders when he connects two or more of them. Like other poets, Williams finds the greatest value in using the subjects that are connected, either as equals or in degrees of subordination, by some necessity of his vision, his idea of the world. Beginning with some specific stimulus—a person or thing seen, an action, a situation, an image, whatever—he seeks to show it in its real wholeness, which is to say in a structure of materials and concepts to which it is related. He is limited only by the extent of his understanding and by what he wishes to make, how big or small a poem. These subjects are not arranged as a formal dogma, of course; they exist, tenuously, as concepts nominally different, but possessing that "one-thousandth part of a quality in common" that in Williams' basic vision of the world permits them to be put—demands they be put—in an imaginative order. It is up to the reader to be as little doctrinaire as Williams and to see the new order—and the new concept—that the poem has established.

There are a number of Williams' poems in which he has formed a well-defined pattern of themes arranged in a specific conceptual structure, the best example of which is naturally *Paterson*. But it is probably the very short poem that has caused the most unfortunate misconceptions of Williams' materials and Williams' work. In a poem such as "This Is Just To Say," not only is the underlying subject usually single, but it is so well represented by the materials Williams employs that the reader is inclined to pass the poem off as *purely* observation.

This Is Just to Say

*I have eaten
the plums
that were in
the icebox*

*and which
you were probably
saving
for breakfast*

*Forgive me
they were delicious
so sweet
and so cold* [a354]

What has caught the fancy of so many readers and made this one of Williams' best known poems is the combination of the nature of his materials and his marvelous tone of relish in describing the plums. Few poets (if any) come to mind to whom it would even occur to make such a situation the basis for a whole poem. Yet the true subject of the poem is entirely conventional: the pure joy of the physical life. For all that Miss Koch has said (for other critics as well as herself), "No other poet of our time has made domesticity, the arts of the home, more aesthetically meaningful than Williams," and gone on to call this poem "Williams' masterpiece in this domain," [10] the fact is that domesticity is not what the poem is about, but merely its setting. Miss Koch has been taken in by the strangeness of finding such familiar things and situations in a poem, and she has failed to look far enough to see the basis of Williams' thought. Certainly he makes the domestic scene "meaningful," but only because he has used it to manifest his feelings about a broader field, the essential goodness of enjoyment of the purely physical.

Regarding this one poem, however, the general opinion (which is represented fairly accurately, I think, by Miss Koch) goes at least a part of the way toward finding Williams' ultimate intent—the ideas in the things. It is held off from a fuller understanding by the modern [11] literary schizophrenia. One part of the collective modern mind seeks only the homey, the "down to earth," the *conventionally* simple and "realistic" detail; it finds deep "natural philosophy" in the worst of Frost, for instance, in his snowy woods, his stone walls, his birches, all the paraphernalia of his rustic American *pose*, and ignores the handful of good, toughminded poems that lack this easy sentimentality and sententiousness. The constituents of this group could accept Williams if he would only give them some soft cushion of easy "traditional" homespun philosophy. The other half of the literary mind constantly expects something "deep," something rare, "profound," complicatedly intellectual as the poem's materials; it assumes that the poem's (or poet's) value varies in direct proportion to the degree in which these qualities are present. [12]

These two opinions have been bolstered by the frequent attempts of poets to classify things as inherently either "poetic" or "anti-poetic." Thus, in his preface to Williams' *Collected Poems 1921–1931*, Wallace Stevens did Williams the unintentional disservice of making the distinction and "officially" identifying him with the "anti-poetic." Having first asserted that in order to understand Williams at all one must realize that "he has a sentimental side," presumably meaning a compliment to Williams' sensitivity, after a bit he goes on:

> His passion for the anti-poetic is a blood passion and not a passion of the inkpot. The anti-poetic is his spirit's cure. He needs it as a naked man needs shelter or as an animal

needs salt. To a man with a sentimental side the anti-poetic is that truth, that reality to which all of us are forever fleeing.[13]

Somewhat later Stevens adds: "Something of the unreal is necessary to fecundate the real; something of the sentimental is necessary to fecundate the anti-poetic." [14] To have called Williams sentimental or, as he does at another point, romantic, and to say that as an opposed force the "anti-poetic" is good *for Williams*, does not make whole what Stevens has put asunder. Once it was made, the disjuncture between the apparently mutually exclusive classes remained. What is worse, the opposition of "poetic" and "anti-poetic" seemed to imply that one was positive, the other negative, that one was somehow better and the other worse, especially because of Stevens' specification that the "anti-poetic" was good for Williams, which hinted that it was not good except under given conditions. As a result, Stevens' real intention, to praise Williams' poems, was forgotten, displaced by the factitious distinction.

This sort of distinction is not the product only of the years of the modern *risorgimento*, of course; the poet almost always finds it necessary to determine what words and objects the limiting conventions of his art permit and what they exclude. Looking back at the evidence of the past, virtually all twentieth-century writers have come to two conclusions: that the nature of the conventions is essentially social (perhaps it would be better to say cultural), things acceptable in one time and place being inadmissible in another, and that superimposed upon this general scale of values is the personal one, the sort of self-restriction that Williams finds in Marianne Moore, who will simply not touch on those things that she detests.

Things are in themselves neither "poetic" nor "anti-poetic"; but poetry is a social function not only in its expression of the ideals and knowledge of the society that is its matrix, but in its (primarily inadvertent) reflection of the society's taboos and fears and ignorance. As would be expected, therefore, the best poetry has almost always had the widest range of admissible materials, and the poorest has usually been that for which the "poetic" realm has been most clearly defined and most narrowly limited.

Stevens' notion is all the more surprising and confusing, then, coming as it did when these were the current educated opinions of the poets reacting against the debilitating effects of the taboo-ridden previous artistic generation.

Williams' reaction to such an analysis of himself was characteristic: first an appreciative comment for Marianne Moore's better understanding of his position, through increasingly irritable answers, to a thoroughgoing disgust. In May of 1934, after Miss Moore had reviewed his book (with Stevens' preface), Williams wrote to her:

> Dear Marianne: The thing that I like best about your review of my book is that you have looked at what I have done through my own eyes. I assure you that this is so. Had it not been so you would not have noticed the "inner security" nor the significance of some of the detail—which nobody seems to value as I have valued it. [d147]

A year and a half later, in another letter to Miss Moore in which he thanked her for liking "An Early Martyr," he remarks:

> There is a good deal of rebellion still in what I write, rebellion against stereotyped poetic process—the too meticulous choice among other things. In too much refinement there lurks a sterility that wishes to pass too often for purity when it is anything but that. Coarseness for its own sake is inexcusable, but a Rabelaisian sanity requires that the rare and the fine be exhibited as coming like everything else from the dirt. There is no incompatibility between them. [d155–56]

In 1948, however, when the general acceptance of Stevens' dichotomy had become unbearably evident after fourteen years of hearing the distinction made not only about his materials but about his versification, and especially about his use of prose in *Paterson,* Williams wrote to Horace Gregory "Frankly I'm sick of the constant aping of the Stevens' dictum that I resort to the anti-poetic as a heightening device. That's plain crap—and everyone copies it." [d265] In his poems, too he makes his position clear. "And they speak, / euphemistically, of the anti-poetic! / Garbage. Half the world ignored . . ." [b24] This is the frontal assault, the fundamental statement; but all through the poem, "To All Gentleness," appear the things in which his idea lives and manifests itself: flowers. "Out of fear lest the flower be broken / the rose puts out its thorns. That / is the natural way." [b24] Or, again:

> *The flower is our sign.*
>
> *Milkweed, a single stalk on the bare*
> *embankment (and where*
> *does the imagination begin?*
>
> *Violence and*
> *gentleness, which is the core? Is*
> *gentleness the core?)*
>
> *Slender green*
> *reaching up from sand and rubble (the*
> *anti-poetic they say ignorantly, a*
> *disassociation)*
>
> *premising the flower,*
> *without which, no flower.* [b28]

Precisely this kind of meretricious, spurious dissociation of things is one of the ideas he has in mind when he says, in *Paterson*, "Divorce is / the sign of knowledge in our time, / divorce! divorce!" [e28] For Williams, knowledge must not be compartmentalized; if the poem is to be made up of useful knowledge, as Williams thinks it must, then the world must be shown in its wholeness: not only the "poetic" materials acceptable to the conventional proprieties, but that other part that lies—or moves, fights, makes a mess—immediately around us in our humdrum everyday lives. The two parts are indivisible: ". . . Rolling / up! obverse, reverse; / the drunk the sober; the illustrious / the gross; one." [e12] Or, rubbing our noses in it, as he says in the delightful "Fragment" (a title with its own wonderful ironies):

> *My God, Bill, what have you done?*
>
> *What do you think I've done? I've*
> *opened up the world.*
>
> *Where did you get them? Marvellous*
> *beautiful!*

*Where does all snot come from? Under
the nose,*

Yea-uh?

*—the gutter, where everything comes
from, the manure heap.* [a453]

(It is important to realize that Williams does practice
what he preaches: he refuses to divorce the "serious" from
the amusing. He is not stuffy about poetry; it is a part of
life in the here and now, not something sacrosanct,
possessed of an innate self-seriousness. For him it is too
important to be merely serious. Perhaps that is why he
always refuses to talk about Poetry and insists upon
talking about poems.)

Essentially Williams' argument comes to a statement to
which Eliot and Pound (if not Stevens) would give their
assent: nothing is inadmissible to the poem *if the poet
shows it a significant part of his poetic world.* Unfortunately for Williams' readers, however, he never identified
himself with any formalized program for or against
anything that would give them a handy scale for judging
significance: he is neither a communist nor a Catholic, a
fascist nor an anarchist (at least not a bomb-throwing
anarchist-by-doctrine), an esthete nor a materialist, nor is
he even (that last resort of the unsatisfied seeker for some
sort of authoritarian order) a homosexual. This is not to
say that he has no definite attitudes toward his world or
ideas and ideals, but merely that one cannot judge his
materials by others' standards. He puts this to the reader
as an image of the actual world and his cryptic comment
upon it in the poem entitled (with delicate irony)
"Pastoral":

*When I was younger
it was plain to me
I must make something of myself.
Older now
I walk back streets
admiring the houses
of the very poor:
roof out of line with sides
the yards cluttered*

> *with old chicken wire, ashes,*
> *furniture gone wrong;*
> *the fences and outhouses*
> *built of barrel-staves*
> *and parts of boxes, all,*
> *if I am fortunate,*
> *smeared a bluish green*
> *that properly weathered*
> *pleases me best*
> *of all colors.*
>
>   *No one*
>   *will believe this*
>   *of vast import to the nation.* [a121]

What will not be believed of vast import (positive as well as negative) is not the mere fact of poverty, but the things *as things:* these are the "anti-poetic," the objects that he claims are virtually impossible to lift to the imagination because they are so "close to the nose." For all its seemingly oracular final remark, the poem is not a socio-political comment prognosticating the depression of fif-teen years later; rather, it is a half-humorous, wryly plaintive comment upon the conventional values of his society, upon the discrepancy between the "official" nature of things and their real nature. He has learned that if examined for their own intrinsic qualities, these objects unrecognized "officially" as anything but the products of social failure can be found physically beautiful in them-selves as well as evidence of our common humanity.

With another sort of material that Williams uses the problem is the same, but his reasoning may at first be more difficult to see. This is the object for which we have an active dislike or distaste. For Williams feels (as so many artists of the past fifty years have felt) that it is sometimes necessary to use the extreme simply for its shockingness—that when the poet cannot move his reader gently, by normal means, he must disgust him, anger him, surprise him enough to destroy conventional attitudes. Yet in this, too, Williams' practice remains based on his conviction that there is no "anti-poetic"; while he intends to shock, he will not falsify and claim for his materials values that he does not believe they possess. For example there is his poem "Perfection."

O lovely apple!
beautifully and completely
rotten,
hardly a contour marred—

perhaps a little
shrivelled at the top but that
aside perfect
in every detail! O lovely

apple! what a
deep and suffusing brown
mantles that
unspoiled surface! No one

has moved you
since I placed you on the porch
rail a month ago
to ripen.

No one. No one! [b40]

The extremeness of this poem lies not in its language, its
"plain speech" (which is not so plain. "contour,"
"marred," "suffusing," "mantles"), but in the particulars
of actuality that are its world. For here again is material
that on the face of it seems hardly the matter of a poem—
and yet why not? Even in rottenness perfection remains
perfection: the color is, as Williams indicates, a beautiful
deep brown, which is surely not intrinsically inferior to
red or green; the surface is as smooth as it was a month
before; the shape has not altered significantly and is still
pleasing. Regarded as a physical entity, then, regarded as a
thing *seen*, dissociated from the usual consideration of its
food qualities, the apple is logically an excellent example
of perfection. In this sense Williams is accepting the
thing for what it is; he does not consider it as food
because by the change of its physical nature it no longer *is*
food. He does not make of it what it is not, that is, but
accepts it as a pleasing physical form rather than as a
disgusting perversion of what it *had been*. Williams
knows as well as we, though, that we cannot cut ourselves
off immediately from attitudes and reactions that have
entered the very grain of our being; his joy and his esthetic
gratification startle us despite their obvious sensibleness in
terms of his data and despite our presumable willingness

to see with his vision. Yet even this conflict started in our minds is a sufficient result; we cannot return completely to the old view of the world. Our vision has been clarified and the power of our perception of reality (which is to say our imagination) has been intensified.

This portion of Williams' "theory of the poem" can explain a great deal about what seems, often, either Williams' inability to treat "large" problems with intelligent seriousness or a social, intellectual, and artistic perversity so great that he just cannot resist thumbing his nose even in his most sober moments. The fact of the matter is that if the reader ignores the supposed difference between "poetic" and "anti-poetic" and attempts to accept things for what they are in the context of the poem, he will find not only that he is generally able to see what Williams is about, but that the materials are with rare exceptions sensible and proper. Williams is trying to measure and thereby define and describe his world as it is, not as it might be.

His world is not merely the corner of New Jersey in which he happens to have been born and to have lived, and from which he chooses most of his materials; he is in no sense a regionalist. Not only did he say in the privacy of a letter to Pound, "You talk like a crow with a cleft palate when you repeat your old gag of heredity, where you come from or where I come from. Do you really agree that place matters? Or time either?" [d69] Earlier he had written in the prologue to *Kora in Hell* that he wished to state "how little it means to me whether I live here, there or elsewhere or succeed in this, that or the other so long as I can keep my mind free from the trammels of literature. . . ." [c13] And in another letter to Pound, in 1933, he asserted, "I know as well as you do that there's nothing sacred about any land. But I also know (as you do also) that there's no taboo effective against any land, and where I live is no more a 'province' than I make it." [d139–40] He is looking at the whole world and defining it in terms of his experience and the things he knows first hand, through the senses. The corollary to his dictum "no ideas but in things" is his statement "the local is the universal." [d223]

Like every other part of Williams' poetic theory, this idea becomes the subject of a poem. In "The Men," for example, Williams demonstrates the equality of physical conditions between Moscow and Passaic and concludes that the men of Moscow or Warsaw are different from the men of Passaic not in kind, but in the conditions of their minds, in vision. Moscow's "dignity" is greater than Passaic's only in that "A few men have added color better / to the canvas, that's all." [a459] And we, in turn, believe what he says about Moscow and Warsaw because we know his basic reference, Passaic—or another city that from our experience corresponds to Passaic—and our imaginations apprehend the universal in the here and now. Williams knows that he can and must write only as a product of that time and place in which chance has put him—"in the American Grain." He does not suppose any more than Chaucer or Wordsworth that because of his "local" materials his poems are of value solely in the locality of their place (or time). On the contrary, he believes that *only* with those local materials whose actual existence he knows completely, familiarly, can he transcend the immediate and approach universality. This is something, he said in 1944, that "I have been saying for a generation: There is no universal except in the local. I myself took it from Dewey. So it is not new." [d224] But it is also something that has its roots in his idea that all changes but art, which is always alive by virtue of its sensuality, of which locality is a necessary condition.

> Being an artist I can produce, if I am able, universals of general applicability. If I succeed in keeping myself objective enough, sensual enough, I can produce the factors, the concretions of materials by which others shall understand and so be led to use—that they may the better see, touch, taste, enjoy—their own world *differing as it may* from mine. By mine, they, different, can be discovered to be the same as I, and, thrown into contrast, will see the implications of a general enjoyment through me. [c197–98]

It is in this matter of where to seek the poem's materials that Williams differs most from poets such as Eliot and Pound, who conceive of their art as being comprised not of first-hand experience alone, but equally (sometimes one would suspect even *primarily*) of what they have experienced in reading. (This includes nonartistic literature: sociology, anthropology, theology, history, economics, and so forth.) Williams is not at all anti-literary, as his critics would have us believe; actually, as is evident from poems such as "Raleigh Was Right," his work has frequent literary allusions, assumptions of inferred knowledge of past art on the part of reader, echoes of other poets. One encounters, for instance, such literary-myth references as the Orpheus theme in *Paterson:* the poet having come to an identification with the dog, and Orpheus being the archetype of poets, Williams creates a three-way identity in which the dog (poet) drowned in the river (identified with time, history, and with language) becomes an echo of Orpheus—and all poets (who are all people) who have no language to save them, drowned out by the broken words of the populace, "the great beast," [e70, 84, passim] as Orpheus was drowned out by the bacchantes.

The reader will also come across seemingly offhand borrowings and rephrasings: "and a white birch / with yellow leaves / and few / and loosely hung. . . ." [a301] or "But where shall we go? / We cannot resolve ourselves / into a dew / nor sink into the earth." [b22] Here the use of Shakespeare's sonnet and the line from *Hamlet* are obvious enough, as Williams intends they be; where he feels it proper—that is, where he believes the material to be a sufficiently integral part of the general knowledge of educated men—Williams uses such borrowed bits and pieces for their immediate effect. But we have been made accustomed in our time (in good part by Pound and Eliot) to a sort of intellectual-artistic acrostic puzzle in which not only are the often abstruse references and allusions of primary importance as things, as materials, but it is essential to any comprehension of the poem to attribute them accurately to time, place, and author, and even, at times, to a specific work. Williams always tries to make them of secondary importance, using them for the most part in such fashion that they have intrinsic values as parts of the poem even for the reader who does not know their literary significance; the specific reference is necessary only infrequently, as in the poem in which he is writing directly about an artist or a specific work. Even in a poem such as "The Dance," which attempts to translate the visual qualities of Breughel's "The Kermess" into verbal qualities, one can not only understand but enjoy the poem without having seen the painting. More than anything else it is this openness in his use of literary materials, this assumption that they are only another part of normal experience, that has caused many readers to overlook what is there and assume his lack of interest in past art. Essentially, Williams is literate, not literary.

In effect (though not formally or explicitly) what Williams has done is to conceive of the materials of the world as being divided into three classes of existence: the human, the natural, and the mechanical-constructs. Outside of this division there exists art—in a sense of a higher kind of being because of its immutability, its reflection of reality in its ordered structure of things, its "sensuality." But it is the three classes of things found in the everyday world of actuality that make up the poem, and it is with these that one must concern himself first of all.

The human realm is the world of people and their personal, direct relationships—the realm of all the emotional, intellectual, and physical qualities that form that unique animal, a *man*. But Williams does not see men as an integrated part of the second class, the natural world; that is composed of all the *other* naturally created things, whether animate or inanimate. Coming between the two classes and thereby helping to disrupt the needed (and theoretically normal) contact and harmony between them, is the third group, a strange product of man's purely rational powers, containing all *made* things, from dog leashes to skyscrapers, from tin cans to cities. Everything thus falls into one class or another and is by definition excluded from the others—unless the imagination sees the common quality that places them in the order of the "imaginative category."

Certainly this sort of classification of things is not new; in fact, it is one of the fundamental assumptions of most Romantic poetry. It would not be of importance, therefore, except for one condition: Williams' absolute conviction that such fragmentation is innately and completely evil. His attitude (which is the matter of the following chapter) is simply that this is the way things *are*, not the way they should be—that the separation, the divorce, of one thing from another in our time is a fact that the poet must deal with if he is to find new structures that reflect reality. Thus one finds a poem such as "Raleigh Was Right," with its basis in men's separation from the natural world, or "The Horse," in which Williams very carefully interrelates the three realms by simile.

> *The horse moves*
> *independently*
> *without reference*
> *to his load*
>
> *He has eyes*
> *like a woman and*
> *turns them*
> *about, throws*
>
> *back his ears*
> *and is generally*
> *conscious of*
> *the world. Yet*
>
> *he pulls when*
> *he must and*
> *pulls well, blowing*
> *fog from*
>
> *his nostrils*
> *like fumes from*
> *the twin*
> *exhausts of a car.* [b89]

What is of particular interest here is not the stated physical likeness of the horse and the woman, although that starts the mind in the right direction by an easy, obvious step. It is the implied categorical similarity, first, between horse and man in consciousness of the world and in doing what has to be done, and, second, between the horse and the car. The last is most impressive, because Williams has reversed the familiar, conventional order of defining the mechanical in terms of the natural; this turnabout surprises the reader and so makes a strong, sure bond of similarity. And yet why should this new order not be the usual? Which object is better known in our society? Williams has begun with two assumptions: (1) that in poems we still think of the natural as the familiar and the mechanical related to it, whereas in reality the reverse is true; (2) that we consider natural things and mechanical things as discrete. And he has proceeded to perform the poet's traditional service of defining the unfamiliar in terms of the familiar by showing previously unperceived relationships. He is not attempting merely to show the two things' similarity, however; he is trying to get at the horse's uniqueness, its whatness, by describing for the moment its important qualities. He does this by showing the qualities in terms of objects representative of two classes in which, nominally, the horse does not have any place, but which objects typify for us the important qualities of consciousness and power. If Williams is successful in doing this, not only does he make the nature of the horse clearer, but he establishes a partial order (structure) of supposedly unlike things that helps to evidence the underlying unity of the world.

Fortunately, Williams does not often make the dissociation of things an emphatic explicit concern of the poem; as in "The Horse," this decisive condition of our life is implied by the way in which he orders and associates his materials. Obviously, "no ideas but in things" again. Yet as one of his basic assumptions about the nature of the world it is also quite naturally one of his primary structural methods. It lies at the bottom of such long poems as "The Sea-Elephant," for example, in which the sea elephant, having been removed from the natural world in order to be displayed not even as a representative of that world, but as a mere curiosity, unrelated to anything, becomes identified in the poem with love, which for Williams means life in its wholeness. Thus is the natural taken from its own world and put into an alien place where it is not valued for what it is or for its relationship to us, but for its apparent *un*relatedness, its difference its *only* quality. To which Williams' answer is:

> *Yes*
> *it's wonderful but they*
> *ought to*
>
> *put it*
> *back into the sea where*
> *it came from.*
> *Blouaugh!* [*a*72–73]

One finds Williams' assumption of the separation of the three "worlds" also as the implicit basis of many short poems, where the value of Williams' vision lies precisely in his ability to show us the falsity of our usual attitudes toward things. Especially where we least expect to find a quality common to the natural realm and the mechanical-construct, Williams does find one, as in "Between Walls":

Between Walls

the back wings
of the

hospital where
nothing

will grow lie
cinders

in which shine
the broken

pieces of a green
bottle [a343]

In a letter to Babette Deutsch in 1948, Williams remarked, "There's nothing very subtle about the poem; all it means, as far as I know, is that in a waste of cinders loveliness, in the form of color, stands up alive. Epicurus meant something of the same." [d265] But what makes the loveliness truly significant is the apparent relationship through color of the green bottle to the green that will not grow; the beauty of the made thing replaces and stands for the natural.

Ultimately, of course, in *Paterson*, the poem in which he has attempted to unite and articulate fully all his beliefs about both the actual world and art, Williams presents the dissociation of things as the primary evil in the world. Here, where a man is a city and the city paired with, but separated from, the fecundating giant female counterpart, the mountain and her natural world, the divorce is stated: men from nature, from what they have made, and from each other. Not only are the three classes of existence broken apart, but even within them things are separated. And the language that might save men, might make them (and the world) whole again, is divorced from the things it represents, just as it is gone from men's mouths.

IF WE ARE to understand at all what Williams is about in his poems, it is imperative that we keep in mind his repeated assertion that poetry—and especially American poetry—is not now at one of its flowering points. There are times, he says, when the materials and the techniques of the poem have been assembled, refreshed, matured, and "the final summative artist arrives" who draws together all the separate elements into a great efflorescence of poems—"and makes it necessary for men to begin inventing all over again." [c103] Williams sees himself as a beginner, a builder toward that point, who must experiment, invent: he is the root of that new (and New World) branch that will flower—sometime. In 1932 he wrote to Kay Boyle:

> Though there is no clear perception of poetic form today and though there can be none until the poem itself appears as the rule in fact, yet it is silly to make a mystery of the pre-masterly period. It is a period without mastery, that is all. It is a period in which the form has not yet been found. It is a formative time whose duty it is to bare the essentials, to shuck away the hulls, to lay open at least the problems with open eyes. [d133]

Twelve years later he had come to a somewhat higher valuation of the achievements of his time; but his general concept remained, unaltered. In a note to Stevens he remarked:

> You know, it makes me think that we do begin to have an elder group who are, in fact, in themselves, a critique

and a *vade mecum* of an art that is slowly acquiring reality here in our God-forsaken territory.

It will later generate an assembler who will make the history. [d229]

In the light of this idea, it is understandable that so much of the time Williams should think of the world in terms of the poem, and especially in terms of the primary needs of the newly born *American* poem of the twentieth-century *risorgimento:* suitable language and structures. Specifically, this constant involvement with the problem of how to make a new, viable poetry causes him often to think of nominally social, political, and moral issues primarily as they affect the making of the poem. Confronted with a specific situation or experience, he *may* see it in terms of its direct effects upon men, but he is as likely to see it in terms of its effects upon the poem. Because the poem is for him the one true means of transmitting useful knowledge without distortion, he believes that whatever affects it necessarily affects men indirectly. In the end, therefore, he has a moral scheme based at least as much on esthetic values as on the purely social, and if at times this makes for a poetry too self-centered, too concerned with the problems of its own being, with its own nature, such a scheme also creates a marvelous unity of values. There is no need to apologize for anything that the poem will admit but that conventional moral codes will not; there is no necessity to force upon the poem's materials a scale of values that has no bearing upon them. Neither the old orthodoxies nor the new, science and its socially deterministic offshoots, have anything to do with Williams' poems except as materials like any others that he finds about him in the world—they are conditions of our lives like the weather or the qualities of the ground we live on.

In this respect Williams comes very close to Pound's (early) idea of the morality of art deriving from the accuracy of its representation: "Bad art is inaccurate art. It is art that makes false reports." [1] Art is not concerned with any religious moral code or scheme of philosophical ethics; like science, Pound felt, art is objective. "Yet it takes a deal of talking to convince a layman that bad art is 'immoral.' And that good art however 'immoral' it is, is wholly a thing of virtue." [2]

Because of these convictions, Williams' intent in his poems is first of all to *show* things—to describe them, in a sense to "name" them. This is a fact impossible to make too plain or repeat too often. Whatever else we may say about his view of the world, we must first recognize that overriding all other considerations in the making of a poem is his belief that the poem must show the reality of things; while obviously he must—and does—have definite attitudes toward specific aspects of the world, the expression of these personal particular desires and aversions is subordinate to the need for expressing *how things are*. In a talk given at the University of Washington in 1948 and published in his *Selected Essays* under the title "The Poem as a Field of Action," Williams said:

> And let me remind you here to keep in your minds the term reality as contrasted with phantasy and to tell you that the *subject matter* of the poem is always phantasy— what is wished for, realized in the "dream" of the poem— but that the structure confronts something else. [c281]

What it confronts—and presents—is the structure of reality, as manifested both in the patterns of language (speech) available to the poem (which is Williams' immediate concern in the essay) and in the orders of the particulars of reality, the materials. Williams is thus making the distinction between the conceptual *subject* of the poem—the poet's "dream"—and what he must use for his *representation*. These are for Williams the only constituents of the world of the poem; philosophy and metaphysics have no more to do with poetry than does sociology, or any other mode of knowledge. They are different forms of knowing, and they only burden the poem.

In a letter to Norman Macleod in 1945, Williams tried to make clear what the focus of his life had been:

> . . . I know that whatever my life has been it has been single in purpose, simple in design and constantly directed to the one end of discovery, if possible, of some purpose in being alive, in being a thinking person and in being an active force. The purpose in my "composit" is never clear or has never been made clear. Oh well, that's to be found by the critic, not me. I know my own difficult answer and it is not to be put into words—but work.
> Poetry, an art, is what answer I have. [d238]

His specification of poetry as "an art" is significant because it is intended to establish the answer's independence; the poem is sufficient unto itself.

> So that when I say, and some well-meaning critic attacks my intelligence for saying it, that art has nothing to do with metaphysics—I am aiming at the very core of the whole matter. Art is some sort of an honest answer, the forms of art, the discovery of the new in art forms—but to mix that with metaphysics is the prime intellectual offense of my day. [d238–39]

As a result of this belief Williams has produced a poetry free from any extrinsic intellectual system. It is impossible to approach his work via a formal body of beliefs or any other external information, whether biographical, historical, or whatever, except to clarify an occasional specific reference. His attitudes, those products of the interplay of his rational "ideas" and his nonrational responses to his surroundings that form his poems' subjects, cannot be defined from the outside in. Yet if one listens at all to Williams' strictures regarding how a poem should be made, he must also see that Williams has given him a corresponding method for understanding it. What must be kept in mind is that in Williams' poems, his letters, his essays—in his every comment on the art—he has insisted upon the "making" of the poem: the poet does not merely "write" or "create" a poem, he *makes* it. This difference of terminology is more than a semantic quibble; it is Williams' way of asserting not only that the poet is not merely an unwitting agent for social forces unknown to him, but, above all, that he is not "inspired" in the modern psychological translation of the term—his unconscious does not merely set loose from the depths of his frustration ideas and emotions that of themselves find their symbolizing words and orders and settle upon the heretofore blank page as poems. As he remarks in the Author's Introduction (1944) to "The Wedge."

> It is an error attributable to the Freudian concept of the thing, that the arts are a resort from frustration, a misconception still entertained in many minds.
> They speak as though action itself in all its phases were not compatible with frustration. All action the same. But Richard Cœur de Lion wrote at least one of the finest lyrics of his day. [b3]

As Williams conceives of it, the poem is as much the result of deliberate, conscious action as the physical structure of a ship or a victory in battle; it is the immediate product of all the qualities of the poet's mind as his will directs their labors.

The process thus seen, it is evident that whatever its origins, the poet's choice of specific subjects and materials is nonetheless a *choice:* he uses one thing rather than another because he believes it for some reason the better stuff of which to make the poem. Ideally, everything in the poem must have its purpose and its reason for being.

> To make two bald statements: There's nothing sentimental about a machine, and: A poem is a small (or large) machine made of words. When I say there's nothing sentimental about a poem I mean that there can be no part, as in any other machine, that is redundant.
>
> Prose may carry a load of ill-defined matters like a ship. But poetry is the machine which drives it, pruned to a perfect economy. [h4]

Always implied, then, is the answer to why any given thing is in the poem: if the reader considers what is given and how it is presented, he has the evidence he needs to determine *why* it is there, the nature of the poet's attitude of which it is a manifestation. For what is important to Williams is *what is there*, what the poet has made—its structures, the natures of the materials as represented by language. If the poem cannot stand by itself with the strength of its own "life," the poet has failed to use his art well: the poem is insufficiently "made." The ideal poem for which Williams strives is a completely self-sustaining entity; to understand it, from literal surface to most tenuous implications, the reader does not have to have any special knowledge, as he must for many of Pound's and Eliot's poems. And in actual practice, for his venture into Williams' poems he need be equipped with nothing more than a fundamental literateness and—most important—a willingness to go where Williams takes him and to look at what Williams has made with as much understanding and imagination as he possesses.

An illustration of this approach to the poem can best be made by looking at one of Williams' less well-known poems, "Fine Work with Pitch and Copper."

> Now they are resting
> in the fleckless light
> separately in unison
>
> like the sacks
> of sifted stone stacked
> regularly by twos
>
> about the flat roof
> ready after lunch
> to be opened and strewn
>
> The copper in eight
> foot strips has been
> beaten lengthwise
>
> down the center at right
> angles and lies ready
> to edge the coping
>
> One still chewing
> picks up a copper strip
> and runs his eye along it [a368]

The substance of this poetic world is simple and common-place: roofing materials (ground stone and copper), a roof being worked on, men to do the work—and "the fleckless light." But the title hints by the use of the word "fine" that this ordinariness cannot be *all* there is to the poem; "fine" is clearly a statement of value judgment. In Williams' poems—as in Stevens'—the title is often a crucial statement of the poet's attitude and intent, really an integral part of the poem. It must therefore be that somewhere in the manner of Williams' presentation of the materials there is something deserving of notice and consideration.

There is, of course. To begin with, there is the indefiniteness of "they" in the opening line. The reader is confronted by an indeterminate number of undefined objects (though they are presumably animate, since they are "resting"); the number never clarifies, but the reader's guess that they are the men necessary to do the work proves correct—yet only in the last stanza, after their harmony with the inanimate world has been established. Following the mysterious "they," the phrase "The fleck-less light" serves to magnify not only the resting objects, but the whole picture, by virtue of its perfection, its rarity: it is a perfection of the air such as one sees in early Renaissance painting and one that we have all experienced at one time or another, a light that washes, cleans, clarifies everything. One can recall this experience and reproduce it in his imagination. Thus the ideal order exists in the harmony of the regularly placed pairs of sacks and the similar separateness in unison of the men, and this perfection is supported both by the ideal quality of the light and by the preparedness of the materials and the resting men.

In addition to the various images of perfection that reflect and reinforce one another, there is the image of precision in the fourth and fifth stanzas. The details of this flatly literal statement imply a considerable degree of difficulty and exactitude in the work that has been done on the copper; the length of the strips, the preciseness of the term "right angles," and the specification that the bend runs down "the center" define the nature of the work. And these, too, lie ready to use, materials with which to make the job a perfectly completed whole. Everything in the poem works toward the same end.

Only in the final stanza does any action occur. But after the five stanzas focussing upon the static quality of preparedness in the ideal orders, the action is one that the reader does not expect: with everything waiting for "after lunch," instead of delaying until the lunch time ends and forces a return to work, "One still chewing / picks up a copper strip / and runs his eye along it." This is the typical gesture signifying a man's pride in his work and his satisfaction *with* what he does and *from* his accomplishment; it is the moment of perfection, of ideality, extended from the static orders of the inanimate world to the actions of the human. The human ideal is *not* to wait, but to continue and extend involvement in the doing. Williams is saying, "Here, look at this. This, too, is rare. This is the way a few men are and all men should be."

It is interesting that in the book *I Wanted to Write a Poem,* in which Edith Heal arranged a chronological bibliography of Williams' writings annotated by Williams' conversation with her (a wonderful sort of running monologue) about what he had been doing and thinking as he wrote each book, Williams says of "Fine Work with Pitch and Copper."

Yes, this was a time [1936] when I was working hard for order, searching for a form for the stanzas, making them little units, regular, orderly. The poem "Fine Work with Pitch and Copper" is really telling about my struggle with verse.[3]

What is significant is that although this may have been Williams' intent and his own "meaning" for the poem, it is only a limitation of the poem-as-it-*is*, and it is, therefore, irrelevant to the reader's "meaning." Instead of seeing the actions of the everyday world in terms of the making of poems, Williams has thought of the poem and the act of making it as represented by nonpoetic things and labors; he has reversed his usual process. But the poem is not merely symbolic of something other than what it says. It tells about his "struggle with verse" only in its typicalness of *all* men who take price in their craft, their hard-worked-at skills. This typicalness is precisely the value of the last stanza, the omission of which would make the poem completely pointless—in fact, not a poem at all. One could probably work out a point-for-point correspondence between the facts of the poem and the facts of Williams' life and labors—the regularity of sacks and stanzas, the separation within a connecting order, the getting up from lunch and the writing between patients' visits to his office, and so forth. But this would only tell us something about Williams, whereas what we want (and need) to know is something about men; we *expect* a poet to struggle with his craft, to seek perfection always and to find his greatest satisfaction in it, but to discover these things as an inherent human condition suddenly apparent in the everyday world and in "ordinary" men is to extend our understanding of our own potentialities.

This complex image of harmony among the various kinds of existence in "Fine Work with Pitch and Copper" is an illustration of the one fundamental attitude that runs through virtually all of Williams' poems—the evil of the dissociation of things and the corresponding need for unity. More than anything else Williams has sought to find a wholeness in existence, a state of being in which will come the harmony among the mechanical, the natural, and the human worlds of which "Fine Work with Pitch and Copper" is a paradigm. The images of such a wholeness are indistinct in some poems, subordinated to the immediate focus—the specific subject of the poem; in others they are the true subject, sharply defined and clearly what is important. But for obvious reasons Williams cannot often find a single image of the actual world that displays perfect correspondences among all three "worlds"; as a result, except in the long poems, where he has enough room for series of juxtapositions, the poem generally identifies only two directly, with the third an adumbration, its suggested correspondence supported by Williams' own faith in his vision of the real interrelatedness of things.

Though undoubtedly not among Williams' best poems, "The Motor-Barge" and "The Mind Hesitant" are in the clarity of their intentions nearly perfect examples of his concept of the underlying oneness of the world. In "The Motor-Barge" Williams constructs a complex image; relying upon denotative statement and apparent literalness rather than the associations of metaphor, he chooses from his observation those details that make an accurate replica of his actual world and of the order in which its mechanical and natural elements are related.

> *The motor-barge is*
> *at the bridge the*
> *air lead*
> *the broken ice*
>
> *unmoving. A gull,*
> *the eternal*
> *gull, flies as*
> *always, eyes alert*
>
> *beak pointing*
> *to the life-giving*
> *water. Time*
> *falters but for*
>
> *the broad river-*
> *craft which*
> *low in the water*
> *moves grad-*
>
> *ually, edging*
> *between the smeared*
> *bulkheads,*
> *churning a mild*

wake, laboring
to push past
the constriction
with its heavy load. [b92]

The point of relationship between the barge and the natural realm that makes the poem more than merely a descriptive set-piece is, of course, the statement about time. Up to this comment upon what the poet sees, everything is still, the motor-barge, the bridge, the air, the river ice all related only by the harmony of their motionlessness; even the gull, though it "flies," is "the eternal gull" that we see hovering or circling without wing movement over every body of coastal water—and motionless in the mind, too, in the fixity of its purpose. But with the direct statement about time, a new perception appears: by the motion of the motor-barge we recognize the similar meaningful motion of the ice-burdened river; the difficulty of progress for each parallels the other and parallels also the gull's constantly difficult search for food in "the lifegiving / water." The river (one of Williams' favorite poetic objects) thereby supports both the natural world and the mechanical product of the human. In so doing, it assumes the character of time. But time is a purely human concept, and the mention of it suggests the relatedness of what is seen to the human world that sees it. Also evidencing the connection with the human is the implicit necessary relationship of the mechanical objects to the men who made and use them and to the minds from which they were born (the river taking on, by the most tenuous of implications, a correspondence to thought, too). To sustain the whole impression of universally difficult progress, the structure of the poem is such that movement is constricted and arduous; statements and even words are split and carried through line ends and ends of stanzas, so that in the necessity of often reading several lines to get the whole image or idea, the movement of the poem is slow and by direct progression from one thing to the next, centripetal, toward unity.

"The Mind Hesitant" also uses the river as its means of unification, but between the human and the natural worlds. Just as the association of a river with time in "The Motor-Barge" is not in itself a new or unusual idea, the identification of the river with the human mind in this poem is a familiar poetic device. The source of the poem's freshness of perception is in its particulars, the metaphors that compose the unifying identification, and in the *manner* of Williams' statement of the first metaphor.

> Sometimes the river
> becomes a river in the mind
> or of the mind
> or in and of the mind
>
> Its banks snow
> the tide falling a dark
> rim lies between
> the water and the shore
>
> And the mind hesitant
> regarding the stream
> senses
> a likeness which it
>
> will find—a complex
> image: something
> of white brows
> bound by a ribbon
>
> of sooty thought
> beyond, yes well beyond
> the mobile features
> of swiftly
>
> flowing waters, before
> the tide will
> change
> and rise again, maybe [b118]

In this poem Williams establishes the point of relationship immediately; but what appears at first to be a conventional form of metaphor develops into something unusual. By the qualifications of "or of the mind / or in and of the mind," the river maintains its objective existence outside the mind as well as its assumed image-life within. In fact, the stanza becomes, finally, a literal statement of what happens: that at times a man may imaginatively project himself into the world about him and identify hiself with it—not as poetic metaphor, but as psychological fact. With this establishment of the nature of the imagination as its foundation, the mind can become the center of the poem from which to view the things external to it, and at the same time it can use its very consciousness of self to establish the identity between itself and them. Thus instead of the mind being described in terms of the river, actually the river and its surroundings are anthropomorphized, the snow-covered banks, the soot-dirtied ground, the water itself all becoming a replica of the mind as it sees itself and its enveloping physical features. In this fashion Williams accomplishes the ambivalence that he believes is the basis of the "imaginative array"—the revelation of the quality-in-common within the uniqueness of each thing. For if the mind is hesitant, the water has its tides, too; but the tides of the water *will* rise, surely, regularly, in their predictable pattern of flux and reflux, while the tides of the mind "will / change / and rise again, maybe."

The attitude tht makes possible both "The Motor-Barge" and "The Mind Hesitant" is one of the typical characteristics of contemporary poetry: it is at once a reaction against and a product of the Romantic concept of the opposition of nature and our industrial society. This is not to say that organized society is a *direct* concern of either poem—any more than it is an explicit or direct concern of more than a very small percentage of Wordsworth's poems. Rather, its relative value is an integral part of the whole structure of thought without which Williams'—or Wordsworth's—expressed attitude toward nature alone would be neither significant nor sensible; from this basis of belief in the mutual opposition of the two stems Williams' search for underlying correspondences in a fragmented world and Wordsworth's desire for a *return* to nature and the wholeness of the "simple" rustic life. Thus Williams' division of existence into three "worlds" is empirical, not ideal; this is his conception of the way twentieth-century men generally regard things and as a consequence have made their world. It is certainly not what he wishes, nor even what he believes an unavoidable state of affairs; on the contrary, he sees wholeness both as the ideal and as the unrecognized reality of the nature of things. He merely images the intellectual and physical dissociation of things in his time and place.

Yet despite the fact that today the Romantic idea has fallen into general discredit, superseded or at least greatly altered, even among artists, by the scientific "realism" that has become the apparent *Zeitgeist* of our increasingly technological culture, and for all that he would undoubtedly resent the label, Williams' position *is* Romantic. His belief that, from whatever cause, there is a separation and opposition, and his conclusion that the main agent of that disjuncture is the mechanical because it is a product almost entirely of men's rational powers—this is a logical extension in a more highly specialized technological world of the feelings of poets like Wordsworth and Blake.[4] In fact, not only does Williams' work show a still further extension that carries him to the opposition, first, of city and country and, second, of the scientific method (analysis, separation) and the artistic (synthesis, wholeness); it also gives the impression that where the mechanical occurs least, men manage best to find the unity of the world and their place in its order—a truly Romantic idea. The various ages of "reason" have thought of the city's organized society as the ideal expression of the human mind and hence the best possible order of life; it has been the Romantics (of whatever time: Theocritus as well as Wordsworth) who have shifted the ideal order to nature, and in this respect very few contemporary poets—or for that matter nonpoets—have moved far from this central Romantic assumption.

Far more than the evident correspondences of wholeness, therefore, Williams finds dissociation in his world, especially a breaking apart of the human from the natural. But the fragmentation manifests itself not only in the division of broadly general classes; Williams is always interested in the particulars, the detailed actuality in which a man lives, and here, at the level of everyday experience, he sees the process of separation as the most characteristic, most widespread, most permeating evil of the times. What he sees is the so-called "scientific method" of detaching everything from everything else and putting the fragments into mutually exclusive categories as one puts different kinds of buttons into little boxes and forgets that they are all buttons; it is the method of abstraction, and it all tends at last to separate man from man, man even from himself. It is the process of finding the least particle of difference by which a characteristic may be isolated, and as such it is the antithesis of the working of the imagination to find that "thousandth part of a quality in common" by which things may, *in their uniqueness*, be put into relationship and made a replica of the structure of reality. In the end, even words are taken from men, just as (and because) they have been dissociated from what they represent:

> . . . *the language!*
> *—the language*
> *is divorced from their minds,*
> *the language . .   the language!* [e21]

Men are left even without a language by which they can *know*: and just so Williams' words stumble, repeating themselves, often seemingly mindlessly, as they seek a full expression, a way to make a poem.

In the by now too often quoted lines in *Paterson*, Williams puts his case simply and directly: "Divorce is / the sign of knowledge in our time." [e28] "Divorce" is precisely the right word; it indicates not merely a separateness of things, but a wrenching apart of what has been and should be together, a dissolution of the closest, most natural bonds, an isolation where there has been contact, intimacy. This feeling of isolation, of a fragmented world, is endemic in modern poetry. It is, for instance, what made Eliot and Pound leave an America divorced from the European past and seek out a tradition that could hold the separated pieces of times and places and ideas in some sort of unity. It is also subject matter in countless poems—as in "The Waste Land," and it is reflected in the structure of a like number—as in Pound's "Cantos." But for Williams the word "divorce" is especially appropriate in its moral overtones. For this point of divorce is in fact the hub not only from which all his ideas and value judgments radiate, but around which his moral attitudes turn: Williams is nothing if not a moral poet, for whom the greatest possible evil is the distortion of anything from its real nature and from its place in the world. His refusal in his poems to distinguish between the "poetic" and the "anti-poetic" and his attempt to make a true image of the world in a structure formed by a process of accretion are both based in one attitude: his acceptance of all things by the mere virtue of their existence. This acceptance does not constitute approval, implicitly or otherwise; it is the simple recognition that what is, is, whether one like it or not. He does not fall into either of the sentimental views of life and see everything as for the worst or everything as for the best; these excessive attitudes are the products of exaggerated comparison, one thing *opposed* to another in such fashion that acceptance of one forces a rejection of the other. In *Kora in Hell*, Williams warns against such comparisons.

> At the same time it is idle to quarrel over the relative merits of one thing and another, oak leaves will not come on maples. But there is a deeper folly yet in such quarreling: the perfections revealed by a Rembrandt are equal whether it be question of a laughing Saskia or an old woman cleaning her nails.[5]

This tells us two things, one for general application and the other especially applicable to the making of a poem. The first is that we must take things for what they are and what of good they have in them, not by blinding ourselves, Pollyanna-like, to defects, but merely by recognizing virtues whatever and wherever they may be. Williams is saying: delight in the delightful, and don't try to measure it—delight is an absolute. With the second meaning, however, we must go even further, in the world of art particularly. This tells us that we must accept *all* the facts, whether we like them or not, whether they be good or bad; it is the greatest of all evils, Williams implies, to ignore what we dislike and refuse to admit that it exists, or to attempt to alter its appearance by comparing it with things that we consider less or more distasteful. "Be reconciled, poet, with your world, it is / the only truth!" [e103]

This attitude of Williams' toward the acceptance and rejection of the world can be seen even more clearly in the light of its opposition to Eliot's position. Nowhere is the difference between them greater than in their use of concrete details of actuality in the poem: between Williams' delight in things for their own sake and Eliot's permeating passivity, his slightly overrefined taste sickened by the evil in things. This is the opposition of their fundamental attitudes toward life. In good part influenced by Hulme's austere classical vision of man, the severe limitation that Eliot places not only upon the poetic world, but upon the actual, manifests itself in his negative tone, the reflection of his dissatisfaction with the discrepancy between what he sees as the reality and what he wishes as the ideality. Williams feels at least as much desire for a better world, but his ideal, which is just as far from actuality as Eliot's, does not limit his ability to accept the fact of what is. He takes the view that life is not a tragedy, only given *lives* are tragic; tragedy can exist only as a negative quality in a positive world, and the poet must delight in the tragic character's potential goodness in order that the usurpation of the man by evil be significant. Thus, because the extent of man's evil is the shadow of the extent of his goodness, the great tragic poet such as Shakespeare delights in the immensity of the evil in a Macbeth or an Othello. In this same way Williams can delight in anything—not in the nature of its quality (that is, its evilness) but simply in the magnitude of the quality. The pleasure that he finds in viewing the rotten apple in "Perfection" is of this sort. Eliot, on the other hand, can *delight* only in the wholly ideal. F. O. Matthiessen remarks about a passage from the final section of "Ash Wednesday" that Eliot wants to indicate that though in its ascent of the purgatorial mount his spirit "does not want to be distracted any longer by sensuous beauty, still, 'though I do not wish to wish these things, . . .'" the sea, boats, birds, flowers—sights, sounds, and smells—all attract him and his imagination (and memory) cannot help but focus on the physical pleasures of the world. Matthiessen concludes:

> It is impossible to divorce the reflection from the imagery. Exact description of memories of the varied loveliness of the New England coast expresses the very sensation of his distraction, of his turning, in spite of his will, away from the contemplation of God. He is momentarily forgetful of the penance of humility appointed for Ash Wednesday; for he has been lured back to the human realm of desire and loss by the enchantment of the senses.[6]

This quality of mind that Matthiessen describes is diametrically opposed to that of Williams. Eliot does not want to concede that the senses and the things that attract him by stimulating them have virtue. Matthiessen's use of "his distraction" gives the exact sense of Eliot's meaning. The natural emotions and the physical senses of the body desire these things and gravitate toward them, but—as elsewhere for Eliot—the emotions and the senses that engender them are *by definition* inferior to the will and the contemplative mind (reflecting upon God). In fact, the inferiority is such that it becomes at last not just a difference of degree, but an antithesis of values. He is, therefore, turned from the use of the rational, the important, the *good* part, to the animal, the trivial, the *bad* part. Eliot does not in the least mean that the lilacs and the goldenrod and the sea and the rest do not *have* attractiveness; his record of experience is absolutely faithful. But he is dismayed by the seductiveness of the physical world, not only in this one poem, but in virtually all his poems. One might say that for him every day is Ash Wednesday; he wishes he could dissociate himself entirely from "the human realm of desire and loss" and enter the world of the pure spirit.

For Williams the world of the pure spirit is an absurdity: the human world is the whole world of actuality, of physical things, of the emotions and ideas engendered by them, and above all, of action. In contradistinction, the world of the spirit is one in which the mind's opposition to the body is ended; the body does not have to exist because a man is not expected to *do* anything. But it is Williams' conviction that no such opposition *ever* exists—that distinction between the two is specious, since the so-called man of thought is in no way differentiated by nature from the so-called man of action; rather, it is the desire for idea *in* action that is the proper meeting point, the fusion of the two half-men that makes men whole. To repeat one of his statements already quoted:

> They speak as though action itself in all its phases were not compatible with frustration. All action the same. But Richard Cœur de Lion wrote at least one of the finest lyrics of his day. [b3]

This is the basic matter of divorce: the idea that such things are incompatible and must therefore be separated—the act from the thought, those who do from those who know, and finally, the physical from the conceptual—against which Williams has argued constantly in and out of his poems, by precept and by example. For instance, one might look at Williams' "To Ford Madox Ford in Heaven" and his poetic image of Ford in these terms and

compare them with any of Eliot's poems and any of
Eliot's characters. Here is the flesh in all its grossness—
eating, drinking, whoring, and, as Williams imagines,
"wheezing in Heaven" from such exertion of Ford's fat
body. And Williams is delighted to think of the man
translated in his physicality to a Heaven that seems a
projection of the Provençe "he loved so well." The poem
smacks of Rabelais or Chaucer or Shakespeare in Falstaff,
or even of Dante in the *Inferno,* but not of Dante in the
Paradiso, or others of Eliot's more philosophical prefer-
ences; it is entirely human, if not in the formal manner of
academic human*ism.* And it illustrates, not some comparison of *value* between Williams and Eliot, but rather that
when in the preface to his *Selected Essays* Williams picks
out Chaucer, Villon, and Whitman as "Contemporaries
of mind," he does so in good part because of their
attitudes toward this matter of the values of the flesh.
Eliot can *use* fleshly man; but as a true product of
American puritanism he cannot bring himself to accept—
let alone love—man for the imperfect thing he is. If Eliot
loves man, he does so in spite of man's fleshly half; in
effect, he loves one half of each man and is repelled by the
other. Williams loves the man as a whole, but without
blinding himself to the imperfections: these he accepts as
simply part of the inevitable bargain.

More than any of his major contemporaries Williams
has shown a consistent, deep, compassionate regard for
people—any people, all people. He does not divide men
into the saved and the damned. *Al Que Quiere,* published
in 1917, contains a number of poems intended to give
evidence of this ambivalence of nature in everyone, and
these illustrate also Williams' unwillingness to reject even
what is a seeming perversion of humanity without point-
ing out that often our conventional appraisal of the
quality is a mistake. For example in "The Old Men":

> Old men who have studied
> every leg show
> in the city.
> Old men cut from touch
> by the perfumed music—
> polished or fleeced skulls
> that stand before
> the whole theater

in silent attitudes
of attention,—
old men who have taken precedence
over young men
and even over dark-faced
husbands whose minds
are a street with arc-lights.
Solitary old men for whom
we find no excuses—
I bow my head in shame
for those who malign you.
Old men
the peaceful beer of impotence
be yours! [a158]

The Whitmanesque compassion of this early poem has
its counterpart in " 'I Would Not Change for Thine,' "
published some thirty years later; for all that the second
poem is a more elliptical statement—despite the directness of its individual components—Williams' unwillingness to pass any judgment upon the husband and wife is
evidence that his compassionate attitude has not changed.
Their humanity itself presupposes for him a unique
mixture of qualities that one must accept if he is to live
sanely in the world. If that amalgam is a falling short of
perfection—as it must be—so be it.

Shall I stroke your thighs,
having eaten?
Shall I kiss you,
having drunk?

Or drink to you only

—leaving the poor soul
who lives with her husband
(the truck driver)
three months, to spend
the next six
where she can find it,
dropping the kid
of that abandon in whatever
hospital about the country
will take her?

(both have T.B.)

What course has she
to offer at her academy

that he returns to her
each year to listen,
repeated, to the lectures
of her adventures?
And having drunk avidly
and eaten of the philosophies
of their reunion
—tells her his own   .   ?

Happy, happy married pair

I should come to you
fasting, my sweet—you
to whom I would send
a rosy wreath not so much
honoring thee as lending it
a hope that there
I might remembered be. [b174–75]

In effect Williams has always been saying, "Better imperfect but live than perfect but dead." And for this reason he also accepts the fact of change; indeed, one of his fundamental suppositions is that, not only is change an unavoidable condition of life, but the world would be virtually unbearable without it. These are hardly revolutionary assumptions, but they are true and, like all truth, constantly in need of reassertion. Their only possible unconventional aspect in Williams' poems derives from his absolute disbelief in life after death. Death becomes, in his work, no means to a higher glory: " . . . at heart I'm a nonbeliever; nothing makes any difference to me. Death is too real for me to want to become 'dramatic' about it. It claps you between its hands like a flying moth, and you are done: only those who hope find that tragic. I find it simply leaden." [d296] Only life in the here and now is imaginable; he wrote, once, to Marianne Moore:

I decided there was nothing else in life for me but to work. It is the explanation for the calumny that is heaped on my head by women and men alike once they know me long enough. I won't follow causes. I can't. The reason is that it seems so much more important to me that I *am*. Where shall one go? What shall one do? Things have no names for me and places have no significance. As a reward for this anonymity I feel as much a part of things as trees and stones. Heaven seems frankly impossible. I am damned as I succeed. I have no particular hope save to repair, to rescue, to complete. [d147]

Williams cannot look forward, therefore, to the perfections of a heavenly existence and concern himself with that, nor does what he considers the static quality of such a "perfection" appeal in the least to his energetic nature. Death is simply the negation of the all encompassing virtue, life.

It is this concern with and for people as they live their lives—his insistence upon the fact of life in its continual process of change and growth—that creates one disarming quality of Williams' general poetic tone. For Williams' direct acceptive presentation of things *as things* disguises his didactic intent. Miss Koch says in her book on him that section XVIII of "Spring and All" (the section entitled "To Elsie" in the *Collected Earlier Poems*) "represents a didactic impulse of a high order. But it is so deficient in the element of rhetoric which most of us have come to expect in didactic poetry that the finesse of the moral judgment may escape some readers. For, confused by bad nineteenth-century models, we have come to identify the hortatory with the didactic to the detriment of both qualities in modern poetry." [7] As far as it goes, what she says is true, although one has the uneasy feeling that she is thinking of a "moral judgment" in terms of a rather conventional extrinsic morality. But apparently she fails to see that, what is far more important, the didactic impulse is attributable to most of Williams' poems, for nowhere else does she comment on the didactic element in a poem. Nor, in fact, has anyone remarked it. Yet the truth is that Williams is usually didactic, and considering his view of art as a means of transmitting useful information by which men may live a better life, such an attitude toward his reader is inevitable. The apparent contradiction of "usually" and "nowhere else" may be resolved at least in part, however, by clarifying the term "didactic." Not only confused by bad nineteenth-century models as Miss Koch says, but in general under the influence of both the romantic and the puritan traditions, we think of it ordinarily as a synonym for "hortatory." Furthermore, the word is usually construed—as Miss Koch construes it—to indicate a basically Christian "*moral*" instruction. But this definition is obviously inaccurate; it is a restriction to what has been the dominant convention over a given period of time, but it is hardly one appropriate to, say, Greek art, which considered teaching one of its primary duties. Instead, one must understand the word in the broadest sense of "intending to teach." There is a good deal of difference between preaching and teaching. One can teach not only by precept, but by example, and as Pound often does in his poems (if nowhere else!),[8] "Williams uses the latter way. Even so, he has turned a few times to direct instruction by precept (as in "To a Solitary Disciple"), and at least one poem, "Tract," is a first rate work by any standard; in fact, as the title implies, "Tract" is restrained exhortation, but it is not an exhortation toward any external, conventional "morality." [9]

In the short poems, naturally, Williams' didactic intent is most hidden; their very lack of bulk is opposed to the sort of direct argumentation that is ordinarily associated with teaching. They are so clearly occupied with just the fact of being, of presenting their images of things, that this occupation appears the be-all and end-all of their existence. In the long poems—and in *Paterson* especially —the chances for occasional direct address to the reader and for a more complex structure that will give more obvious point to his images make his intent to teach much more apparent; he is able to indicate to the reader without obtrusion, not only what and how things are, but why he has chosen the materials he uses, which is to say, what he would have the reader learn from (or by) them. In "Midas: A Proposal for a Magazine," published originally in 1941, Williams remarks:

> We must know. We must say what we know. We will not be defeated or bemused. But the artist not only knows and reveals, he proves the reliability of his contentions by his works. As with geometry this is the basis of art; the diagram is not didactic. It is fact, proof of the existence of creative man—signed by the creator. [c247]

Williams, too, uses "didactic" to mean "intended to sway the emotions," hortatory; he tries to conceive of the poem as a diagram of truth which the poet merely presents. But the first two sentences tell us something else. They tell us *why* the poet reveals: in order to transmit knowledge—to teach—what he knows and we must all know.

If we grant Williams' central moral concern, his concern with the propriety of all things as they exist naturally (which is after all perhaps the primary concern of every poet), his poems must inevitably be an attempt to show (teach) us the truth, to differentiate for us reality and illusion, things in their real order and the way we understand them (which is to say, often, *mis*understand them) and order them rationally and artificially—that is, the actuality in which we move. This method of teaching is another evidence of the way in which Williams is a true product and reflection of his time; in the best modern tradition, Williams is attempting to teach by showing and to make the reader learn by doing. He would not think of asking complete acquiescence and unthinking reverence on the reader's part for the "authority" of the printed word. True education is for him not a mere process of memorization of the abstractions of a complex intellectual construction; his low valuation of the purely rational process of "knowing" makes that an impossibility. Rather, it is comprised of a knowledge and understanding through the imagination, both of the individual parts of one's vision of reality and of their relationships as the pieces show themselves in the actual world. For this reason Williams is forever saying, in effect, "Look at this and see how important it is—and how (why) it is important to the wholeness of the world."

The prime example of this idea is obviously, again, "The Red Wheelbarrow"—which is itself only a portion of a longer poem, a greater structure. In terms of both his actual world and the poem's world that wheelbarrow is indispensable if their wholeness is to be kept; remove it, and you remove one point where the human, the natural, and the mechanical worlds meet *in harmony*, where the wheelbarrow, its implied user, the chickens, and possibly even the rain have that quality-in-common for which Williams (like ourselves) is always seeking that he may at last form a paradigm—minute, perhaps, but of infinite worth—of the true order of our world. Remove the wheelbarrow, he says, and you remove one of the few measurable, knowable points of reference and fragment the whole into illusorily separated orders.

Williams' didacticism resides principally, therefore, in his intent to correct the evil of illusion by the example of reality—the truth. To put it another way: his intent is didactic in that it would offer useful and usable materials for the government of men's lives. He would undoubtedly agree with Pound's assertion that good art is moral in that it is true, while bad art is immoral in that it is untrue. If an artist gives an untrue picture to his audience, who necessarily expect a true one (upon which to base their actions), then, Williams believes, the artist is guilty of precisely the same sort of immoral act as, say, the politician who gives to the voters an untrue or deceptive picture of a political issue. But for Williams the artist's sin is the greater, for the politician is involved only in the immediate moment and surface of life; his act can almost always be remedied by relatively simple means. The artist, however, is involved in establishing the very basis for *all* action: the vision of reality; and his untruth cannot be corrected except by art of greater *energy*—art that will not only present the true, but displace the untrue from the mind.

It should be clear, then, that though the popular understanding of the terms is inapplicable, the questions of Williams' morality and didacticism are not merely semantic. The truth is that Williams has never been the "simple" (or simple-minded) poet that the common image would have him. References to him such as Miss Koch's remark that "Pieces like 'The Tulip Bed' and 'Blue Flags,' in their dynamic factuality of flowers lead one to agree with Wallace Stevens' dictum that there is no one who writes more exquisitely of flowers" [10] are perhaps true, but they are also irrelevant. Such intended praise is evidence that (to twist the old saying) one can't see the garden for the flowers. At the virtual beginning of Williams' career (1917) Ezra Pound wrote to him in a now famous letter:

> I was very glad to see your wholly incoherent un-American poems in the L. R. [*Little Review*]

> Of course Sandburg will tell you that you miss the "Big drifts," and Bodenheim will object to your not being sufficiently decadent.

> (You thank your bloomin gawd you've got enough Spanish blood to muddy up your mind, and prevent the current American ideation from going through it like a blighted collander.)

> The thing that saves your work is *opacity,* and don't you forget it. Opacity is NOT an American quality. Fizz, swish, gabble of verbiage, these are echt Amerikanisch.[11]

The opacity to which Pound was referring is not, however, the sort produced by a poet's having and using a greater range of knowledge and reference than the reader can come by even with moderate difficulty—that is to say, the sort we find in Pound's own work or in Eliot's. Nor is it the deliberate distortion of the poem's surface—its structure and its language—that we find in the work of a poet like e. e. cummings. Rather, it is the product of Williams' attempt to make his poems moral and didactic without explanation, exhortation, or preaching. His "opacity" is his unwillingness to spell out for the reader what the poem *ought to* mean; it is his determination to make the poem a replica of the actual world from which the reader may learn, by use of the imagination, what complexities underlie the "simplicity" of the materials. Like the world it reflects, the poem is only partly revealed.

One typical example of this "opacity" is "The Bull." Here Williams' fundamental intent is hidden in the virtually perfect unity of the poem as we see it: as it stands, it is a clear picture of a minute corner of the natural world. But what we see as actuality is merely the revealed part of a larger, implied structure. The foundation for the poem—its hidden mass—is Williams' complex of ideas about wholeness and divorce, and thus about good and evil, as well as his desire to show (teach) us the relationship of reality to appearance.

> *It is in captivity—*
> *ringed, haltered, chained*
> *to a drag*
> *the bull is godlike*
>
> *Unlike the cows*
> *he lives alone, nozzles*
> *the sweet grass gingerly*
> *to pass the time away*
>
> *He kneels, lies down*
> *and stretching out*
> *a foreleg licks himself*
> *about the hoof*

then stays
with half-closed eyes,
Olympian commentary on
the bright passage of days.

—The round sun
smooths his lacquer
through
the glossy pinetrees

his substance hard
as ivory or glass—
through which the wind
yet plays—
                    milkless

he nods
the hair between his horns
and eyes matted
with hyacinthine curls [a336–37]

What strikes one immediately about this poem is its quietness. The explosion that seems imminent in the first statement of the bull's captivity never takes place; instead, the poem grows increasingly static as the bull's passivity becomes more and more obviously the focus of Williams' concern. Usually the epitome of raw, wild, passionate strength, the bull here seems, on the contrary, rather like a magnificent huge porcelain figure, removed from us and from all the living world of actuality. He *is* as Williams says "godlike." But in his separation from the cows he has been emasculated—"ringed, haltered, chained / to a drag"; his appearance has been made more perfect, but his purpose (which is to say the reality of his existence) has been perverted. In his sequestration, the bull is an image of the male-principle divorced from the female-principle that it complements and is meant to fecundate.

Seen even in the most literal way, the poem is thus more than one thing: it is a replica of the actual world in which we see the bull for what it is, hard, strong, remote, useless alone, yet beautiful in those qualities; it is an exposition of the perversion of things by divorce and of the evil inherent in such perversion; and by implication it is a statement of the natural wholeness of things, here in terms of sexuality. However, we may consider the bull not merely in its own being, but as a typical example, a

paradigm of all things partaking of the male-principle.
When we do, we find that there are at least two possible
ways other than the literal in which we may understand
the poem's use of sex as subject: as representing men's
direct relationships to each other (in society) and as
representing their indirect relationships to each other (in
art).

The clearest, most overt identifications of sexuality in
Williams' poems have generally been in statements about
art, but until the poems of the 1950's his symbolism had
been rather unsystematic and fragmentary. That is, he did
not try to construct a poem with such completeness of
correspondences as to permit a continual symbolic reading
without hiatuses in which the materials are presented
simply for themselves alone.[12] It is impossible, therefore,
to derive from "The Bull" a perfect point for point
correspondence between the literal statements and the
symbolized comments about art. However, from the bull's
being "ringed, haltered, chained / to a drag" as contrasted
to the inherent freedom of the imagination; from its
sequestration its uselessness (a perversion of reality) and
divorce from the sensual world; and from its milklessness,
implying an inability to sustain life in others, and its ivory-
or glass-like hardness, implying the absence of life itself—
from all this it is possible to infer that Williams associates
the male-principle essentially with the rational faculties
and, by logical antithesis, the female with the imaginative.
(Considering Williams' attitude toward pure reason, such
an association is not surprising.) Furthermore, if this is so,
then Williams is saying—as he so often does—that it is
possible to make a beautiful work of the purely rational,
but it will be sterile, merely decorative, it will be useless as
a means of sustaining our lives because it will be remote
from our actuality: the bull must be set free to mate with
the cows.

If on the evidence of the one poem such reasoning
seems too tenuous and not quite convincing, elsewhere
Williams puts his case in less detail, but more directly. He
speaks at one point of " . . . the thinking male / or the
charged and deliver- / ing female frantic with ecstasies"
[b99] and even as early as 1913, in *The Tempers*, the
poem "Transitional" deals with the subject to much the
same effect.

First he said:
It is the woman in us
That makes us write—
Let us acknowledge it—
Men would be silent.
We are not men
Therefore we can speak
And be conscious
(of the two sides)
Unbent by the sensual
As befits accuracy.

I then said:
Dare you make this
Your propaganda?

And he answered:
Am I not I—here? [a34]

In his later work the sexual representation of the nature of art is a recurrent theme, and often Williams refers to himself as part woman when he thinks of himself as poet. In *Paterson* the poet-sexuality association is a primary element—in the letters from the woman poet to Dr. Paterson; in the Orpheus theme; perverted, in the woman writer in the "Phyllis and Corydon" section of Book IV— her lesbianism a displacement of femaleness by the necessarily sterile assumption of "maleness"; and especially in the wonderful "Beautiful Thing" episode of Book III. Even "the elemental character of the place" is first given in sexual terms: Paterson the city is male; the surrounding mountain with its river and falls that represent (among other things) language is female. The product (and thus the representative) of the rational principle, that is, the city, a construct, is held in the embrace of the imaginative, the natural world. Furthermore, N. F. Paterson is also a poet, but a man, as Williams says, "since I am a man . . . But for all that he is a woman (since I am not a woman) . . . "[13] yet as man-poet constantly in need of the vitalizing intercourse (overtly both sexual and intellectual) with women that we find a major quest in the poem.

What Williams sees, then, in the female-principle is evidently the combination of productiveness (perhaps more properly reproductiveness—the power of maintain-

ing life), acceptance, and gentleness. Like the qualities of
the male-principle as manifested in the bull, however,
they must be fecundated by their complements, strength,
discrimination, and violence (or energy). In a poem such
as "To All Gentleness," therefore, one finds a refusal to
divorce one from the other; Williams says,

> *except*
> *for the gentleness that joins our lives*
> *in one.* [b27]

but later wonders,

> *Violence and*
> *gentleness, which is the core? Is*
> *gentleness the core?*) [b28]

It is art and love (both represented in sexual terms) that
"join our lives," but only as they partake of both their
natural elements, maleness and femaleness, violence and
gentleness, and are thus a part of the actual world.

> *Not the girth of thigh, but*
> *that gentleness that harbors all violence,*
> *the valid juxtaposition, one*
> *by the other, alternates, the cosine, the*
> *cylinder and the rose.* [b29]

It is the ordering of the violence of the world we live in
that makes us whole. Art establishes orders by means of
the imagination, and, maintaining wholeness, it produces
those ideas-in-things that Williams believes the only truly
useful information for ordering the actions—which is to
say, for the government—of men's lives. And it is love, the
source of ideal direct contact between people, that makes
their personal relationships whole.

No matter which way one turns, then, Williams'
ultimate reference for sexuality is to the problem of
"divorce" in our world and its effect upon us. In *Paterson*,
for instance, commenting upon the evil inherent in our
separation of things and our denial of reality, he says:

> . *no woman is virtuous*
> *who does not give herself to her lover*
> *—forthwith.* [e266]

He is not proposing free love or fostering "immorality,"
but asserting, on the contrary, that accepting sexuality as a

necessary element of love is an act of natural morality superior to holding them separate in accordance with the strictures of conventional "morality." For Williams there can be sex without love, but not love without sex; social conventions have nothing to do with the relationship.

An interesting exposition of this matter occurs in "To a Friend Concerning Several Ladies." The simplicity of the desires that he enumerates in the first stanza is obviously more apparent than real: while he does indeed desire the sight of grass and flowers, they are not *all* that he wishes for: sexual desire "comes / between me and these things." Such desire may not be what he wishes ideally, but he cannot escape it—it exists; as a man he can achieve wholeness only through the agency of a woman. But a question arises: what is the relationship of simple physical sexuality to love? In contrast to the orderly simplicity of the natural world imaged in the last stanza, human complexity involves one in a tangle of relationships, often disquieting relationships at that. Obviously Williams is unwilling to accept the romantic notion that he must be "steaming with love" or his sexual drive is purely animal, since to believe this is to divorce one part of man from another. But he is no more willing to propose any equally simple formulation that would answer his question with another hypothesis, another theory: "who can answer these things / till he has tried?" All he can do is break off the consideration and present his image of the wholeness of the natural world—the one immutable reference point and standard for measurement of his own.

If sexuality is only implicit in a poem like "The Bull," most of the time Williams makes it quite explicit; yet his seemingly constant occupation with sex as the matter of his poems is obviously less an interest in the thing itself than in its representational values—which is not to say that Williams has ever ignored its pleasures for their own sake! First of all—though less so now than when he first used it—sex is sometimes effective as shock: in the right context, the stimulus of the supposedly taboo subject forces the reader to drop his conventional attitudes and to see the poem's people and their relationships in terms of Williams' vision. Second, and more important, it is ideally the expression of love, which is what makes possible a statement such as the one quoted from *Paterson*. And finally, sex is the appropriate link between the human and the natural worlds, the one important quality that people have in common with virtually every other living thing.

The last function has Williams' most interesting applications, for it enables him to employ sex with two opposed intents. Where sex is normal, it unites the human and the natural in an image of harmony. But where it is perverted, it becomes a sign of "divorce." Its perversions are necessarily perversions of the human spirit, since by definition it cannot be perverted in the natural world; animals use sex for its own sake, purely, never in order to gain some ulterior goal, whereas men, by virtue of their reason, can employ sex as a means to an unrelated end, thereby perverting it.

Representative of sex in Williams' two antithetical uses of it are, on the one side, such disparate examples as the wonderfully funny observation of "Après le Bain" and the more conventional attitude of "Wide Awake, Full of Love," and, on the other, the grim picture of bitterness and loneliness in "The Raper from Passenack." The first two expose sex as both the motive force and the greatest pleasure of the physical life. In "Après le Bain" the dominant impression is of totally innocent, and therefore normal, involvement with the imagined physical pleasure.

> I gotta
> buy me a new
> girdle.
>
> (I'll buy
> you one) O.K.
> (I wish
>
> you'd wig-
> gle that way
> for me,
>
> I'd be
> a happy man)
> I GOTTA
>
> wig-
> gle for this.
> (you pig) [b196]

All other considerations are for the moment forgotten, both by the people in the poem and by Williams as maker of the poem; only the direct sexual relationship of man and woman is present. But the poem is not obscene, as there is no reason it should be. What remains in the mind is not so much the actual situation, but the underlying propriety of the conversation, expressing as it does the couple's mutual acceptance and affection. The teasing exchange is basically a pleased acknowledgment by the couple that each delights in the other's sexuality and that each is equally delighted in finding himself sexually attractive to the other. Their conversation announces that for the moment the world is for them whole and good.

In a more direct and more conventional way, "Wide Awake, Full of Love" treats the sexual theme not as the act of intercourse itself, but in terms of those physical qualities in the women that "seduced" the speaker. Here, too, the inseparability of sexuality and love is made explicit.

> *Being in this stage*
> *I look to the last,*
> *see myself returning:*
> *the seamed face*
> *as of a tired rider*
> *upon a tired horse*
> *coming up . . .*
>
> *What of your dish-eyes*
> *that have seduced*
> *me? Your voice*
> *whose cello notes*
> *upon the theme have led*
> *me to the music?*
>
> *I see your neck scrawny*
> *your thighs worn*
> *your hair thinning,*
> *whose round brow*
> *pushes it aside, and*
> *turn again upon*
> *the thought: To migrate*
>
> *to that South to hop*
> *again upon the shining*
> *grass there*

> *half ill with love*
> *and mope and*
> *will not startle for*
> *the grinning worm* [b207]

The value of this poem resides in its two or three felicitous phrases and, above all, in the fervent directness with which Williams declares the dependence of love's perfection upon sexual energy; not only does life in general lose fullness by the encroachments of old age, but love itself is no longer complete. This is not to say that love ceases to exist; on the contrary, Williams' expressed desire to regain youth is prompted by his being, as the title says, "full of love" and wishing to have again the chance to express and fulfill it physically, it is another way of showing that for him love *is* life, and the progress of one is representative of the progress of the other: the energy of youth is the sexual energy of love and the sexual appetite is the appetite for the world.

This identification of love and life—perhaps one should say the life-urge, the avidity for all experience—is a constantly repeated concept in Williams' poems. We forget sometimes that for all his writing of the natural world, *his* world—his concern—is fundamentally human. For all that flowers are frequently the materials of his poems—and used with such skill that they seem all his interest—his intent is for the most part that we compare them with our human realm, so often fragmented and perverted from its own natural course. For in his judgment of the world, the great tragedy of our lives is our isolation, our maddening inability in the midst of men to make satisfactory contact with others. If we must make peace with our physical environment, as he says, for instance, in "Raleigh Was Right," we must do so because it will help us to find our common humanity and make peace with ourselves. And thus one finds a poem like "The Raper from Passenack," in which both the man and the raped woman who relates the poem are pathetic results of isolation.

The Raper from Passenack

> *was very kind. When she regained*
> *her wits, he said, It's all right, kid,*
> *I took care of you.*

What a mess she was in. Then he added,
You'll never forget me now.
And drove her home.

Only a man who is sick, she said
would do a thing like that.
It must be so.

No one who is not diseased could be
so insanely cruel. He wants to give it
to someone else—

to justify himself. But if I get a
venereal infection out of this
I won't be treated.

I refuse. You'll find me dead in bed
first. Why not? That's
the way she spoke,

I wish I could shoot him. How would
you like to know a murderer?
I may do it.

I'll know by the end of this week.
I wouldn't scream. I bit him
several times

but he was too strong for me.
I can't yet understand it. I don't
faint so easily.

When I came to myself and realized
what had happened all I could do
was to curse

and call him every vile name I could
think of. I was so glad
to be taken home.

I suppose it's my mind—the fear of
infection. I'd rather a million times
have been got pregnant.

But it's the foulness of it can't
be cured. And hatred, hatred of all men
—and disgust. [a103–4]

The title "The Raper from Passenack" leads one to expect the raper to be Williams' subject, but obviously he is not; yet neither is the girl victim *the* subject. The two people are for the moment united by the act; neither can be seen except as a complement and a function of the other—they exist, in a sense, *only* as they are one in sexual union. Without that union they diminish; together they form a whole, but separately they cease to exist. And after their own fumbling fashion, as Williams shows us, they know this, although they cannot put their feelings into words. The man does not even try; he relies upon action. Therefore, having attempted to break out of his isolation by forcible physical union with the girl, he makes his primary means of reassuring her, not his "It's all right kid, / I took care of you," but the *act* of taking her home. And his assertion that she will never forget him is a *self*-assurance that he has made some kind of lasting contact with another person; it is addressed to her, but directed at himself.

Having established the man's situation, Williams turns to the girl's case, and with surprising results. Her first remark, that only a man who is sick could commit the act, develops into her *idée fixe* that his sickness is not mental, but physical, that he wishes to give her a "venereal infection." "He wants to give it / to someone else— / to justify himself." That is precisely what he does want, but what he wants to give is *himself*, not a venereal disease; his act is a desperate attempt to justify his humanity that has been denied by his isolated existence. She is thus the ideal complement to him in her refusal to eradicate all the traces of their contact by having the presumed disease treated. Instead, she considers an act psychologically (and socially) equivalent to his—murder. For she is as sick, mentally, as he. She, too, needs to assert her existence, to make an impression that will draw others' attention: "How would / you like to know a murderer?" Her acquiescence during the rape, her "faint," her refusal to scream, her (knowingly) futile, evidently passionate, biting—all these are the unsatisfactory attempts on her part to make contact. She is "so glad / to be taken home"—*by him!* In the end her monologue reveals the state of mind that she has always had, in her relations with all men, though she is thinking presumably only of him: it is the fear of infection that disturbs her, not the fear of pregnancy; it is the foulness not just of rape, but of sexuality itself. "And hatred, hatred of all men / —and disgust." This is the expression of the ultimate isolation in our world. Sex is associated with disease, it is dirty, it is to be separated from our lives—but men, *all* men, force its foulness upon women. The female-principle is divorced from the male, and as a result they are both sterile; instead of creating, they destroy.

This sterility of perverted love and perverted sexuality dismays Williams. He is not bothered by men's transgressions of conventional morality; in fact, it is his opinion that such morality leads for the most part to those very perversions. Part I, the "Phyllis and Corydon" section, of the fourth book of *Paterson* is the perfect example of Williams' concern. In a letter to Marianne Moore he said of it:

> The form, an idyl of Theocritus, a perverted but still recognizable "happy" picture of the past, is there. It is a sad picture today. It shows a desire to achieve all that we most hope for in the world. We all share the world together, we none of us possess it to ourselves. We WANT to share it. Only because we are thwarted do we fail to achieve our release. But as poets all we can do is to say what we see and let the rest speak for itself. [d305]

The perversion of the idyl is brought about in several ways, the most important of which are, first, Corydon's being a lesbian and a cultured city dweller, and, second, the inability of Phyllis to give herself to anyone—to the lesbian Corydon or her lover Paterson, or to *any* man. The section is a complex image of sterility. Yet there is no "moral" judgment by conventional standards. As Williams wrote to Robert Lowell:

> Especially the ladies don't like to hear one of their sex mentioned in any but a genteel light; it infuriates them to be told that the Lesbian exists and has a perfect right to exist without their feeling that they, as women, have been denigrated. . . . I like the old gal of whom I spoke, she was at least cultured and not without feeling of a distinguished sort. I don't mind telling you that I started writing of her in a satiric mood—but she won me quite over. I ended by feeling admiration for her and real regret at her defeat. [d302]

But she *is* defeated; the potential love in her is held off
from realization by the inescapable fact of its distortion
from physical normality. In answer to Phyllis' question
whether she had ever been to bed with a man, she says
matter-of-factly, yet with evident sadness,

> Good Shot. With this body? I think I'm more horse
> than woman. Did you ever see such skin as mine? Speckled
> like a Guinea hen. [e187]

She is cut off from contact by the physical, while Phyllis,
her complement, is physically desirable, but unable in her
insensitivity and inhibition, as a product of "the more or
less primitive world of the provincial city," [d304] to *give*
herself sexually to Paterson (who is in his way equally
impotent).

> *Why do you torment yourself?   I can't*
> *think unless you're naked.   I wouldn't blame*
>
> *you if you beat me up, punched me,*
> *anything at all   .   I wouldn't do*
>
> *you that much honor. What! what did you say?*
> *I said I wouldn't do you that much*
>
> *honor   .   So that's all?*
> *I'm afraid so.   Something I shall always*
>
> *desire, you've seen to that. Talk to me.*
> *This is not the time for it. Why did you let*
>
> *me come? Who knows, why did you? I like*
> *coming here, I need you.   I know that   .*
>
> *hoping I'd take it from you, lacking*
> *your consent.   I've lost out, haven't I?*
>
> *You have.   Pull down my slip   .*
> *He lay upon his back upon the couch.*
>
> *She came, half dressed, and straddled him.*
> *My thighs are sore from riding   .*
>
> *Oh let me breathe!   After I'm married*
> *you must take me out sometime.   If that's*
>
> *what you want   .   [e199–200]*

What Phyllis wants is both in its basic brutality more primitive than Corydon's desires, and in her romantic desire for the spurious glamor of the stolen fruit—to be taken out after she is married—a pathetic result of the isolation of our society.

It is this movement away from the wholeness of love, the exclusion of parts that are by nature integral to the whole relationship, that was Williams' increasing concern over his last thirty-five years or more. As he grew older he wrote more and more of the need for—and the perversions of—love. And although love takes on in his poems additional meanings as the prime motive force in the world, although it becomes significant of the acceptance of life, of experience, because it is the most elemental, most intimate and direct mode of making contact with the life that is outside us, Williams never loses sight of its essential sexuality, even when he must at last say that for an old man the purely physical gratifications are past.

Williams' insistence upon love's centrality to our lives is thus both a desperate plea for a more constant, deeper, and more openly direct contact between men—and between men and the natural world—and an equally desperate affirmation of goodness (beauty) as the reality of the natural and human worlds. Clearly a product of his partaking of the Romantic spirit (though whether cause or effect of his youthful "apprenticeship" to Keats would be pure speculation), his idea has been to create the identity of beauty and goodness: whatever is beautiful is good, whatever is good is beautiful. But Williams' standards of beauty and goodness are as a consequence different from the commonly accepted, and they are often difficult for the reader to accept, simply because the reader does not really understand them. Williams has on occasion gone so far, even, as to deny the validity of the word "beauty."

> But how is truth concerned in a thing so ghostlike over words as style? We may at least attempt to say what we have found untrue of it. To a style is often applied the word "beautiful"; and "Beauty is truth, truth beauty," said Keats; "that is all ye know and all ye need know." By saying this Keats showed what I take to have been a typical conviction of his time consonant with Byron's intentions toward life and Goethe's praise of Byron. But

today we have reinspected that premise and rejected it by
saying that if beauty is truth and since we cannot get along
without truth, then beauty is a useless term and one to be
dispensed with. Here is a location for our attack; we have
discarded beauty; at its best it seems truth incompletely
realized. Styles can no longer be described as beautiful.
[c75]

What Williams has done is not, as he says, to discard
beauty, but to discard the word. He has found it too
encrusted with connotations of past conventional attitudes, too associated with merely a (for him) meretricious
prettiness and with outworn proprieties to be useful in his
world. At another time, again speaking of the past, he
wrote:

> There was then a subject matter that was "poetic" and
> in many minds that is still poetry—and exclusively so—the
> "beautiful" or pious (and so beautiful) wish expressed in
> beautiful language—a dream. That still is poetry: full stop.
> Well, that was the world to be desired and the poets
> merely expressed a general wish and so were useful each in
> his day.
> But with the industrial revolution, and steadily since
> then, a new spirit—a new *Zeitgeist* has possessed the world,
> and as a consequence new values have replaced the old,
> aristocratic concepts—which had a pretty seamy side if you
> looked at them like a Christian. [c282]

The result of this new spirit is a beauty-in-ugliness—like
the rotten apple in "Perfection." It shocks us, as it is
supposed to, since Williams' intent is to break out of the
conventional bounds of "beauty" and to expand the realm
of the beautiful, thereby producing more and better
means of contact with the modern world.

His attitudes toward the conventions of beauty are put
effectively in one of his early short poems, "Apology."

> *Why do I write today?*
>
> *The beauty of*
> *the terrible faces*
> *of our nonentities*
> *stirs me to it:*
>
> *colored women*
> *day workers—*
> *old and experienced—*

> *returning home at dusk*
> *in cast off clothing*
> *faces like*
> *old Florentine oak.*
>
> *Also*
>
> *the set pieces*
> *of your faces stir me—*
> *leading citizens—*
> *but not*
> *in the same way.* [a131]

The beauty he sees is both real in itself and a product of his social feelings; it is the unnoticed beauty of the modern actual world as opposed to the conventionally accepted "beauty" in the illusory appearance assumed by the "set pieces."

In direct opposition to the force of love Williams places the organization of society, since restricting individual men's actions is for him, finally, restricting the possibility of men's fulfilling their potential contact with each other. That is, because love is the means of optimum contact between persons and because by definition it is personal, individual, its antithesis is the organization of society, which treats of men as a mass rather than as unique individuals. The result of the organization is, in effect, the "set pieces" of "Apology." While he acknowledges the practical necessity for some sort of regulation in men's lives, he cannot accept the organization he sees, based as it is primarily upon the inherently limited rational understanding. Defining good and evil acts, for the most part, in terms of expediency and usage (conventions), society's organization (government) is to his mind intrinsically pernicious.

This attitude toward society, and its expression in social conventions, he has had since the early poems, and by the time of *Al Que Quiere*, 1917, we find it fully articulated in the poem "Tract." Because it is both an early exposition of an attitude that has not changed and a direct, explicit enunciation of ideas, "Tract" is a valuable statement of Williams' view of the propriety of the natural as contrasted to the impropriety of social convention, of the inherent dignity of men as opposed to the degradation of men by the shams of society.

pretense

In essence, his basic requirement in the poem is that we accept reality and refuse—as he refuses—to make it look like what it is not. He begins with:

> *I will teach you my townspeople*
> *how to perform a funeral*
> *for you have it over a troop*
> *of artists—*
> *unless one should scour the world—*
> *you have the ground sense necessary.*

Having established his belief in their innate ability to act with propriety, he instructs them.

> *I begin with a design for a hearse.*

But his hearse is to be neither black nor white,

> *—and not polished!*
> *Let it be weathered—like a farm wagon—*
> *with gilt wheels (this could be*
> *applied fresh at small expense)*
> *or no wheels at all:*
> *a rough dray to drag over the ground.*

In short, make things natural, let the vehicle represent its content and its function; let it show the erosion of life, with the gilt, applied specially for each use, perhaps to symbolize the wagon's specialness of purpose and the essential goodness of life. And then the afterthought: it might be most fitting to use a dray to convey the mere physical remains to their union with the other clay. From this he proceeds to advise knocking out the glass and to demand:

> *For what purpose? Is it for the dead*
> *to look out or for us to see*
> *how well he is housed or to see*
> *the flowers or the lack of them—*
> *or what?*

Nor may there be

> *upholstery, phew!*
> *and no little brass rollers*
> *and small easy wheels on the bottom—*
> *my townspeople what are you thinking of?*

This the crux of the poem: what is the purpose of each of the elements that Williams condemns? His implied *right from right or normal use*

answer is that they are meant to pervert the appearance of things and to mask reality, to gain the accommodation to ease sought in usual life. He goes on, therefore, to rule out wreaths, and especially hothouse flowers:

> *some common memento is better.*
> *something he prized and is known by* . . . .

The only natural symbol by which we should remember the man is that which truly represents him in his individuality: we must not distort his image. And finally Williams gives the instructions for the driver and the mourners: take the driver down and make him walk inconspicuously—he is only a function of the corpse. As for ourselves, we must

> *Walk behind—as they do in France,*
> *seventh class, or if you ride*
> *Hell take curtains; sit openly—*
> *to the weather as to grief.*
> *Or do you think you can shut grief in?*
> *What—from us? We who have perhaps*
> *nothing to lose? Share with us*
> *share with us—it will be money*
> *in your pockets.*
>   *Go now*
> *I think you are ready.* [a129–31]

It is obvious that as in so many other poems the basis here for all of Williams' objections and advice is his belief that the conventions of our society are forces for isolation, for the senseless divorce of things. This is not to say that Williams is either simple-mindedly blind to all else or single-mindedly a victim of an *idée fixe*, but that running through all his work there is necessarily a fundamental pattern of ideas that directs his vision. Especially in the poems of some length and complexity these ideas are delineated thoroughly by his use of various materials; yet while each particular is unique, it cannot but take color from Williams' general cast of mind. Hence, for instance, his ideas about art must parallel his ideas about society, at least in terms of general standards. As a matter of fact, "Tract" could be worked out almost perfectly as a symbolic statement of advice to the artist regarding the practice of his art. It begins by advising the artist not to be arty, or an artist before all: be a man first, an artist second. Next, in the design for the hearse, it warns against using borrowed forms and advises a rough naturalness, a form that will represent the actual world. Third, Williams says: don't ,use the "hothouse flowers" of "poetic" language, use the natural idiom. Then, as a continuation of the idea, he proposes avoidance of the easy but false "poetic" clichés and conventional, artificial metaphors: use true "mementoes"—actuality—as symbols. Going further, he contends that the poet *as poet* is unimportant and should not be discernible—the poem is what matters, nothing else. And he concludes with the advice to be open to experience and to make it available as useful knowledge.

Whether Williams ever intended a symbolic interpretation even vaguely like this, one must doubt. But whether he did or not is really beside the point. What matters is the fact that even if wholly a product of the reader's ingenuity, such a reading does no violence to the poem's literal social meaning; on the contrary, it reinforces the obviously social sense, of which poetry is for him but "another sector of the field."

Williams puts his attitude toward society in various other particular terms, though at bottom they too must come to the same concept—divorce. Not only do laws and other such external regulations separate people, he asserts, but the complexity of society, its specializations and fragmentations even by occupation, as well as by class and color and beliefs, isolates us from our common humanity. But above all, it is modern society's most typical product, the city, that acts as the disuniter. Williams finds this doubly unfortunate because it is also the city that he sees as the expression of modern man's dreams; for all his anger at its evils, he discovers a beauty and a grandeur in the skyscrapers, in the bridges, in all the massive structures that he regards as a true modern reflection of human potentials.

Because he does consider the city at least in part good, he can use his duality of feeling, for instance, in making the identification of city and man in *Paterson*, the diversity of the city's elements imaging the limitless possibilities of the human spirit, both for good and, perverted, for evil. At the poem's outset he announces:

> *Paterson* is a long poem in four parts—that a man in himself is a city, beginning, seeking, achieving and concluding his life in ways which the various aspects of a city may embody—if imaginatively conceived—any city, all the details of which may be made to voice his most intimate convictions. . . . [e,author's note]

Yet perhaps Williams' ambivalent feelings show themselves more clearly in less ambitious poems where, simply because of the impossibility of qualifying and refining his attitude to indicate all its shadings in so brief a space, Williams takes a clearer, more positive position. Each representation is less precise in itself, but it contributes to the final composite. Thus he can refer tenderly (and very much in echo of Whitman) to "the moody / water-loving giants of Manhattan" [a164] or in "Perpetuum Mobile: The City" he can write, with just a hint of his reservations:

> > *—a dream*
> > *we dreamed*
> > *each*
> > *separately*
> > *we two*
>
> > *of love*
> > *and of*
> > *desire*
>
> > *that fused*
> > *in the night—*

and then

> > *a dream*
> > *a little false*

finally ending his thought with

> > *a dream*
> > *toward which*
> > *we love—*
> > *at night*
> > *more*
> > *than a little*
> > *false—* [a384–85]

Not only as itself, but also as it represents modern society, the city is a dream or an illusion in two senses: as

we see its beauties expressing our desires and as we refuse
to see the ugliness of much of its reality, its perversions of
the human spirit. For Williams goes on in the poem to
give pictures of two armored-truck guards who themselves
hold up the bank and drive off with the money—"For
love!"; of the brutalities of being

> *Dragged*
>   *insensible*
> *upon his face*
> *by the lines—*
>
> *—a running horse*
>   *For love.*
>
> *Their eyes*
>   *blown out—*
>
> *—for love, for love!* [a387–88]

and of "Guzzling / the creamy foods" while in the subcel-
lar the hidden waste is

> *chucked down*
> *a chute*
>   *the foulest*
> *sink in the world—* [a388]

These are the broken elements of the city as it maintains
its ambivalent existence.

In "A Place (Any Place) to Transcend all Places"
Williams omits the favorable aspects and goes directly to
the center of his vision of the city's inescapable evil—its
separation from those portions of the world that give it its
life and its pride in artificial distinctions.

> *In New York, it is said,*
> *they do meet (if that is*
> *what is wanted) talk but*
> *nothing is exchanged*
> *unless that guff*
> *can be retranslated: as*
> *to say, that is not*
> *the end, there are channels*
> *above that, draining*
> *places from which New York*
> *is dignified, created (the*
> *deaf are not tuned in).* [b113]

The list of these origins of the city begins with a surprisingly conventional example:

> A church in New Hampshire
> built by its pastor
> from his own wood lot. [b113]

In its ordinariness, however, this image serves to assert once again the difference between the artificial construct divorced from its origins and the organic whole in which the natural and the human move in concert. For as Williams has said, "the city depends, literally, both for its men and its materials on the country, . . ." [d225] The rest of the list is more typically Williams and—at least as presented—less conventional, but it is at all times meant to show wholeness in one form or another: a rose, a couple in the sexual act, the leaves on a tree—the natural and human worlds. Only after this premise has been set firmly in the reader's mind does Williams describe New York, but the details of the description are uninventive, a bit shopworn: mass-uniformity, subways, sweatshops, and so on. He concludes,

> —and we have
> :Southern writers, foreign
> writers, hugging a dis-
> tinction, while perspectived
> behind them following
> the crisis (at home)
> peasant loyalties inspire
> the avant-garde. [b114]

Artistically this poem is Williams at his worst, but (and in good part because) it is Williams at his most specific intellectually. It is a statement in poem-form of one of the central ideas in his essay "The American Background": that the primary culture of a country is a product of men's contact with the physical nature of the place and that in America the city has embodied a secondary culture, one that had no such contact to give it vitality. At one point in the essay he concludes:

> The cities had at least population and a quickened pulse, but in getting this, as in everything where the secondary culture predominates, the cost was severe. It involved the actual decay of the small community. And the decay of the small community was a primary cultural decay. It would

seem as if the city has as its very being the raising of the cultural level, as if it were in the very stream of the great flow. Quite the opposite is true, unless the place of the city, as a sort of turntable and that only, be clearly realized. [c147]

As usual, in the poem he is both conventionally liberal and cantankerously unconventional: his description of the city and his (sentimentalized) vision of the rustic church are precisely the sort of terms employed often during the twenties and thirties to declare the liberal reaction to the pressures and degradations of city life. As he has shown in his poems and maintained in his letters and his autobiography, he has never been attracted to either the radical or the reactionary dogmas; the proof here of this aversion is his typical, odd, interesting comment clinching the argument about the evils of the city—the reference to the writers divorced from place and from the true proportions of reality and "hugging a distinction" as their lone, last means of being noticed. In this, he is his own obstinate, cantankerous self reminding us also of the excesses that some of us overlook because for us they are excesses "on the side of the angels."

The specific reasons for Williams' inability to make this particular poem better than it is we cannot establish, but there is a very considerable generic similarity between its least valuable portions and other poems in which he deals directly with immediate and specific political or social "problems"—like "Impromptu: The Suckers," "And Who Do You Think 'They' Are?" and "Jingle." They, too, fail as poems, for the most part; they, too, lose sight of "the radiant gist" [e218] in their involvement with the pain of the moment and their focus upon the transient— though not for that any the less painful—immediate causes of the distress. The difficulty Williams has at such times is simply that, as he himself has constantly asserted, he is not interested in politics *as such*. In a letter to Babette Deutsch in 1947, for example, he said:

> I have found little I wanted to say about the labor violence which has had Paterson as its scene during the last thirty or, perhaps, hundred years. You found "The Strike." Good. You will find more in the prose of *Life Along the Passaic River*, especially the first account contained therein. However, in *Paterson* the social unrest that occasions all

strikes is strong—underscored, especially in the 3d part, but I must confess that the aesthetic shock occasioned by the rise of the masses upon the artist receives top notice.

In Part or Book II . . . there will be much more in the same manner, . . . much more relating to the economic distress occasioned by human greed and blindness—aided, as always, by the church, all churches in the broadest sense of that designation—but still, there will be little treating directly of the rise of labor as a named force. [d258–59]

He is interested in his human world as a collection of individual men, not as classes or groups—and certainly not as abstract categories like "workers" or "the unemployed" or any other escape from the unpleasantness of knowing life as it is lived. Yet, as we know, the contemporary world is the hardest to make a poem of—the closer to the artist and the reader (perhaps especially the reader, who is always slower to make the jump from actuality to the inner reality),[14] the harder is the material to shape into art —the less it is workable under the heat of the imagination. As Williams put it:

. . . the thing that stands eternally in the way of really good writing is always one: the virtual impossibility of lifting to the imagination those things which lie under the direct scrutiny of the senses, close to the nose. [c11]

When Williams becomes involved in matters of immediate but transitory importance, therefore, he is usually unable to bring them up to the level of the imagination precisely because they are too "close to the nose." That is, while his theory of the poem demands their use *as is*— social-political acts produced by unique conjunctions of specific causes—his real concern is not with *this form* in which the problems are manifested, but with the underlying human motives and more or less universal human qualities that are demonstrated in the actions of individual men. These "political" poems seek the same end as the non-"political" poems, but they are unsuccessful because they deal with society in terms of the wrong specifics and lack generality of concept; they are inextricably tied to the merely topical materials that belong, like much of Eliot's religiosity, to a different mode of thought and expression. The result of such a conflict is virtually inevitable: the topical remains, as undigested experience and even of less value than if Williams had had some more fully articulated, more doctrinaire social or political system into which to fit the materials and some specific program for political action to promote.

This is not to say that Williams can never use such materials so that they are of value to the poem. In many poems, where the informing subject is clear and strong enough, the social or political asides imbedded in the larger matrix do serve as representative examples of universals. And infrequently, too, there is a short poem in which the topical materials are so subordinated to other matters that they serve to heighten the impact of these others, perhaps by the very contrast between them. Such, for example, is the short poem "Song," in which each kind of statement supports and sharpens the other.

> *Russia! Russia! you might say*
> *and furrow the brow*
> *but I say: There are flowers upon*
> *the R.R. embankment*
> *woven by growing in and out among*
> *the rusted guard cables*
> *lying there in the grass, flowers*
> *daisy shaped, pink*
> *and white in the September glare.*
> *Count upon it there*
> *will be soon a further revolution.* [b208]

Or there is the sort of poem in which Williams' reference to the contemporary socio-political phenomenon is more implicit, though none the less real. "The R R Bums" had its origin in the depression of the thirties, but it is not restricted to that particular social context for its meaning.

> *Their most prized possession—*
> *their liberty—*
> *Hands behind a coat*
> *shiny green. Tall, the eyes*
> *downcast—*
> *Sunlight through a clutter of*
> *wet clouds, lush weeds—*
> *The oriole!*
> *Hungry as an oriole.* [b155]

Williams has done in both poems what he does so often, perhaps what he succeeds with best: he has taken bits of two worlds—here the human and the natural—and in juxtaposing them shown by similarity and contrast how what occurs in one implies what happens in the other. This is not, however, the same sort of primary political (or "social") work as the unsuccessful "Figueras Castle" or "A Fond Farewell" among the short poems, nor is it like the more successful but ultimately unsatisfying long poem "Impromptu: The Suckers," which is carried along in the main by the power of the anger that seeks expression but can never quite find adequate embodiment in word or image. Neither is "Song" more than superficially related to "Choral: The Pink Church," which does juxtapose its various social images and ideas against each other, occasionally with great beauty and force. Rather, it is like "The Horse" (discussed earlier for its kind of materials) and "The Motor Barge" and "The Mind Hesitant," in which Williams' intent is to bring together the dissociated natural, human, and mechanical worlds.

But if Williams is in no way a writer of "social protest" as a political instrument, he is on the other hand—as we know so well by now—dedicated to "Americanness" in poems. He has condemned as dangerous nonsense Eliot's well-known contention that place is only place and contended that, on the contrary, "The local is the universal." [c73] However, as he reminded Pound in a letter as late in their friendship as 1933, "Fer the luv of God snap out of it! I'm no more sentimental about 'murika' than Li Po was about China or Shakespeare about Yingland or any damned Frog about Paris." [d139] Rather, like any good artist, looking for the imaginative perception and understanding of reality, he remarks in an essay on Marianne Moore that just as in geometry lines at angles to each other establish points of intersection, in poetry the lines of vision established by situating oneself here or there establish points of penetration to the underlying reality, to understanding what is. Hence, the local "is merely a variant serving to locate some point of . . . penetration." [c122]

Only, therefore, in the particularity of the local, the completeness of the microcosm that the poet knows thoroughly, can he avoid artificial separations. If he can establish in the reader's mind the concept of the wholeness of any one place, the poet can cause the reader to see that this idea applies as well to larger areas and at last to the world as a whole. To think of Williams—as so many people have thought of him—as a poet of New Jersey, or of the eastern United States, or even of the nation as a distinct, discrete, if somewhat patchwork, whole, is to miss the point of his work completely, just as those readers miss it who think of him as "American" in the way that Carl Sandburg is "American." Williams is as different from Sandburg as he is from Eliot. He deplores effusions over Chicago or wheat fields because they happen to be part of an abstraction called America (of which by a legal technicality he is that abstraction a citizen) as much as he abhors an escape from those wheat fields and that or any other city—even from citizenship. Both he can see only as a flight from the unpleasantness and difficulty of actuality into abstraction—sentimentalization and unrealistic assertion that the only truly American is the midwestern on the one hand, and forced historical continuity and a theoretical literary tradition on the other.

Williams himself has given the best possible explanation of his position. Speaking of culture, he says flatly:

> It has to be where it arises, or everything related to the life there ceases. It isn't a thing: it's an act. If it stands still, it is dead. It is the realization of the qualities of a place in relation to the life which occupies it; embracing everything involved, climate, geographic position, relative size, history, other cultures—as well as the character of its sands, flowers, minerals and the condition of knowledge within its borders. It is the act of lifting these things into an ordered and utilized whole which is culture. It isn't something left over afterward. That is the record only. The act is the thing. It can't be escaped or avoided if life is to go on. It is in the fullest sense that which is fit. [c157]

The job of the poet is thus to make available knowledge of these several aspects of the nature of the place, thereby reflecting the culture and changing it, recreating it. The making of poems is both the making of the record and the continuation of the "act." If the poem is local in the right way, then, it will seek not merely its things' quaintness, but their relationships to each other and to the rest of the world; as a product of locality in time and place, it will maintain a wholeness, a sensuality, a life.

In order to fulfill these needs of the poem, one of the things Williams has tried to achieve in making an American poetry is the creation of a new myth, even a whole new mythology, as some of the other American poets, such as Robinson Jeffers, Stephen Vincent Benét, Edgar Lee Masters, and Hart Crane, have tried to do. These others have generally turned to historical or folk heroes, impatiently refusing to await the characters' natural ripening into literary materials, and such attempts have failed precisely because the characters' public lives have been so well "documented" as to prevent the modern reader (who is nothing if not a believer in "objective"—or "scientific"—truth) from suspending disbelief in their equally detailed fictional adventures. Williams, however, has created in his own poetic world—and in particular in *Paterson*—an original, independent, perhaps even too private myth supported by the logic of his vision and, especially, by the sort of objective-scientific observation of phenomena, natural and otherwise, that the twentieth century expects as the shape of "truth." He, too, has borrowed from history, but primarily the forgotten, the unpopular; many of his "borrowings" are, in fact, purely imaginary, like the imitations of old records that he intersperses with the real records in *Paterson*, but they are dressed in such factual style as to make them appear fact. And he has also gone to folk legend for sources, but again only to use the little known, the alterable, and the local (like Sam Patch in *Paterson*).

It would not be an injustice to Williams to say that Williams' occupation with his kind of myth is, like the occupation of so many others with the standard myths of antiquity, a reflection of our loss of a viable popular literary tradition and a deep concern over that loss. He differs with the traditionalists, however, on the valuation of the ancient myth. He wrote to Frank L. Moore:

> The myth wearies me. We never learn. We crave the often repeated, to do over and over the same thing. Because an event happened in the past, we think that our lives too somehow partake of it; anything to give us a sense of reality. We think that because it happened once upon a time, it must be so. [d296]

Myth is in his use of it the expression of the common-consciousness—that is to say, of the shared understanding and the shared attitudes toward shared experience. It is not a look toward the past, but, as for the Greeks, the self-image of an area's culture (in Williams' meaning of the term); as such it acts, ideally, as the built-in psychic balance that neutralizes the pressures of actuality and preserves sanity—it is art developed to its broadest acceptability and utility. Furthermore, our experiences are to some degree different from the old ones—we have different specific needs, dangers, modes of action, knowledge—and they are shared by a greater number of people. The basic human patterns cannot change appreciably, of course, but the variations in the immediate forms of experience and attitude are great enough to demand a correspondingly more varied, more comprehensive expression than was either necessary or possible for the traditional small society like the Greeks'.

As a result of all this, Williams finds it necessary to give his readers the raw experience as well as the distilled epitome; not only in the long poems but in the short, he must show us our world of actuality precisely, even clinically, often at great length and from many directions, so that he can make comprehensible his insight into reality. In this regard, however, *Paterson* is necessarily the prime example as well as the best product of Williams' mythopeic method; in the shorter poems there is insufficient scope to permit the necessary development of the intended myth, and Williams can do no more than give a name, an act, a situation, the specificality of the reference often nullifying the intent of universality. (This is one reason, perhaps, why so many entirely sympathetic readers do not so much see the poems as individual entities as they see one whole composed of many parts, incomplete in themselves, that blend in memory one with another, a mosaic in which the unity of the whole supersedes the individuality of any single piece.) But in *Paterson* the identification of man with city allows Williams to use his individual—who is not an individual: in his several natures he is rather a fragmented Everyman—as the representative of all men; and his city, which is a continuing actuality in time, is the means of drawing together in one manageable unit all the seemingly disparate threads both of time and of place that he sees, if not actually always coexistent, at least continually converging

and producing an entity (be it man or city) that is at once
unique in the particulars of its actuality and a copartici-
pant with other unique entities in the demonstrably common qualities of their underlying reality. Thus the writers
of the letters in *Paterson,* for instance, can be identified
only by initials (which are at best blank symbols) rather
than by names, which in their unfamiliarity would give
them a restrictive uniqueness setting them apart from
their fellow sharers. It might be argued, of course, that
this complicated and depersonalizing method is unnecessary, the result of inadequacy in the poet, and that he
need do no more than justify in terms of action (either
physical or intellectual) the qualities he assigns his
characters and their universality will be apparent if it is
there. But Williams' intent is not only for the production
and display (or clinical analysis) of a man, or even of
Man, but also for the creation of an image of the place
and the nature of things (physical and intellectual) in the
evolving "act" of culture. He is interested, that is, in
establishment of the common-consciousness.

> For the beginning is assuredly
> the end—since we know nothing, pure
> and simple, beyond
> our own complexities.
>
>   Yet there is
> no return: rolling up out of chaos,
> a nine months' wonder, the city
> the man, an identity—it can't be
> otherwise—an
> interpenetration, both ways. [e11]

He is attempting to do truly what he has said his time
should do—to build, to invest, to refresh and renew for
the eventual summative artist.

In the consideration of time Williams could be said to
conceive of the present as the local in the universality of
history. Only, therefore, through the exact imaginative
understanding of the "now" can the poem represent the
"then." Nothing more divorces us from the world, he
believes, than ignoring the present as the main setting of
the poem; we must live in the present intellectually and
emotionally no less than physically, and an escape to the
supposed authority of the past merely because of its

pastness is neither sensible nor profitable. This is evident from his previously quoted comments on myth. He does not ignore the past, however; if only on the evidence of Paterson, the once prevailing idea of Williams as wholly uninterested in history has fortunately been discarded as thoroughgoing nonsense. But he is not interested in the same way as Eliot or Pound nor is his use of it like Sandburg's or Hart Crane's or Stephen Vincent Benét's.

Of the two approaches to history popular among the poets of his time, one, typified by Pound and Eliot, considers history (or time) a continuum of universals, the applicability to the present of each past act or work of art remaining always constant: The Greeks, the Chinese, the Romans, the renaissance Italians are identical if we can but pierce through to reality, and all their actions are equally pertinent to our developing history, the knowledge of their histories equally useful information and the "facts" in essence interchangeable. In this view *all* that is important is the universality of men's actions (and consequently their ideas and emotions), and this universality has been expressed and differentiated from the purely fortuitous in its time by the literature of the past; it is the duty of the poet, therefore, to restate the prior understandings in such fashion as to identify them with the present and add another step to the progressing continuum. What changes are to be made in the past are changes in terminology, so that the present may be able to comprehend its origins—changes in symbols. But the significance of anything rests in the authority of its repetition: the present idea, attitude, action is validated, ultimately, *only* in its relation to prior existences, all of which are variants or mutations sprung from an archetypal example. The truest expression of this concept is the search for "universal myths," for the recurring legend— *The Golden Bough* its exemplary work and its now basic source book.

The Americanists mentioned above do not so much deny this theory as they limit it and dismiss whatever is not strictly indigenous to the United States. Apparently stemming from Whitman's kind of Americanism, their belief seems to be that we are as a nation so different from others in degree as to have become different in kind; as a result they act as though history is discontinuous when it reaches our shores and anything foreign is by definition almost never pertinent to our situation or useful to us. But the holders of this belief seem not to discriminate among periods or materials within the continental boundaries; for them, too, all the past is equally important (unless it be that one section of the country strikes them as more American than another) and significance is a direct product of pastness.

Between these poles—not alone, surely, but alone among modern American poets of any importance—Williams has attempted to form a sort of temperate zone. He refuses to use history as if antiquity were inherently superior to modernity.

> . . . I have no belief in the continuity of history. To me the classic lives now just as it did then—or not at all. The "Greek" is just as much in Preakness as it was in Athens. Everything we know is a local virtue—if we know it at all—the only difference between the force of a great work and a lesser one being lack of brain and fire in the second. In other words, art can be made of anything—provided it be seen, smelt, touched, apprehended and understood to be what it is—the flesh of a constantly repeated permanence. [d130]

For him there is a *usable* past (a concept he may have taken from his reading of Dewey) in which there are men and things and actions that are related directly to the present, and only by this connection are they given importance. The rest is merely past. The connection is found in the imagination's ordering of things; it is, in other words, what the poet can make of it. It need not be overtly apparent, as the connection between Mrs. Cumming in *Paterson* and the languageless poet is not. It need not in point of actual fact be "American," as the Orpheus-dog-N. F. Paterson theme or the Chinese- and Greek-American correspondences in "Choral: The Pink Church," are not. It need not even be positive, affirmative, but may take the form of an inversion—or perversion—or a negation of the past, the difference implying a continuity in change: blatantly in a poor poem like "The Testament of Perpetual Change," emphatically, as in the "elemental character" and the "modern replicas" in *Paterson*, or more subtly perhaps, as in "Raleigh Was Right." What Williams demands is that there be some organic bond between the representatives of different times; it is the imaginatively conceived structure that contains the authority to indicate significance of either the present or the past. If the poem is well *made*, it will be another evidence of the wholeness of the world—in time, in place, in kind.

One might make a final summative statement about Williams' attitudes and ideas and beliefs by using his comment about N. F. Paterson, doctor, poet, and deliberately to some extent his self-image. Surely, it could describe no one better than it does himself.

> But never, in despair and anxiety,
> forget to drive wit in, in till it discover
> his thoughts, decorous and simple,
> and never forget that though his thoughts
> are decorous and simple, the despair
> and anxiety: the grace and detail of
> a dynamo—[e39]
>
> So in his high decorum he is wise.

This is always the problem for Williams: to find the thought in its decorous simplicity so that we may see the world in its simple decorum.

> Prose may carry a load of ill-defined matters like a ship.
> But poetry is the machine which drives it, pruned to a
> perfect economy. As in all machines its movement is
> intrinsic, undulant, a physical more than a literary charac-
> ter. In a poem this movement is distinguished in each case
> by the character of the speech from which it arises. [b4]

It would be hard to conceive of any more Romantic
description of the poem than this ostensibly anti-Roman-
tic one of Williams' in the Author's Introduction to "The
Wedge." Yet for all its seeming exaggeration it does to a
great extent describe accurately Williams' poems and his
intentions. For Williams is nothing if not a conscious
poet. Unscholarly, antiacademic—even, perhaps, in his life
as a physician, unpoetic—Williams has been, among the
poets of his time, the most constant theorizer about the
mechanics of the poem. Year after year Williams wrote
about contemporary poems and poets, and about his own
wrestlings with the poem, in essays, prefaces, letters,
fragments of any and every sort that form, finally, a
mosaic image of his idea of what a poem is, what it does,
and how it does it.

From this mosaic, however, one concept stands out
most distinctly: the idea of the poet as *maker* and the
poem as a thing *made*. Toward the end of the introduction to "The Wedge" Williams goes on to define the
nature of his identification of poem and machine:

> When a man makes a poem, makes it, mind you, he
> takes words as he finds them interrelated about him and
> composes them—without distortion which would mar their

exact significances—into an intense expression of his perceptions and ardors that they may constitute a revelation
in the speech that he uses. It isn't what he says that counts
as a work of art, it's what he makes, with such intensity of
perception that it lives with an intrinsic movement of its
own to verify its authenticity. Your attention is called now
and then to some beautiful line or sonnet-sequence because
of what is said there. So be it. To me all sonnets say the
same thing of no importance. What does it matter what
the line "says"?

Therc is no poetry of distinction without formal invention, for it is in the intimate form that works of art achieve
thcir exact meaning, in which they most resemble the
machine, to give language its highest dignity, its illumination in the environment to which it is native. [b5]

Clearly it is Williams' belief that like the things and
ideas used in a poem, the form, the structure, of a poem is
a matter of conscious choice; and what a poem "says" is
contained not so much in its overt statement—its philosophy, its doctrine, its "wisdom"—as in how the things are
ordered, how the words that represent the things are made
into a series of relationships. Obviously, therefore, for
Williams the poem must stand in a direct, easily discernible relationship to the language of common speech, it
must partake of that language and not stray too far from
it. At the same time, however, the poem must make
something uncommon of the common, it must formalize
that inherently amorphous mass, must purify it by measuring it, must impose upon the freedom—even irresponsi-
bility—of speech a structure that will reproduce the poet's
understanding of the rhythm, the measured pattern, of
the life of his world. This is, for Williams, the poem's
prime need.

After a brief prose passage in *Paterson, II,* in which
Williams offers a piece of a historical "document," he
returns to a discussion in verse of the indispensability of
poetic invention (see p. 25 for the text of the passage).
While this section is of course concerned with the
functioning and the products of the imagination in
general, even aside from the imagination's particular place
in the poem, it is most directly a discussion of the
problem of the poet's employment and reproduction of
that imagination, that is, the form, the structure, of the
poem. The poet's invention is his reflection of his world,

his measurement of it; it is the thing he has made that expresses, in its movement, in its self-sustained life, the reality that he knows underlies the appearances he lives among. In an essay entitled "Against the Weather: A Study of the Artist," Williams said, "Verse is measure, there is no free verse. *But* the measure must be one of more trust, greater liberty, than has been permitted in the past. It must be an open formation." [C212] While he foresaw—and attempted to create—a kind of verse very different from Eliot's, based upon a conception of reality in turn very different from Eliot's, Williams had no more idea than Eliot of escaping from formal discipline: not freedom *from* measured form, but freedom *for* it was what he sought. He knew that "measure we must have, as long as we are impelled to know complexities of the world about our ears. The verse I envisage, a measure infinitely truer and more subtle than that of the past, comes much closer in its construction to modern concepts of reality." [d332]

These new concepts of reality are what the poet must seek with the changed mind Williams speaks of in *Paterson*; the new measurement of the stars "according / to their relative positions" is for Williams an adaptation in the arts of the Einsteinian theory of relativity, which Williams has long used as a symbol of the modern world and conceived of as the informing intellectual spirit of his time. His new measure, the "open formation," is, therefore, not only the product but the image of our understanding of the universe (human and social as well as physical) as composed of parts only relative to each other; the old forms, the old orders, are based on the belief in absolutes, on a rigidity of all structures, whether esthetic or scientific, social or theological. This is the point at which Williams differs most critically with men like Eliot and Pound, who seek authority in the closed absolutist systems of the past and who, for that reason, were drawn to the past for poetic models.

Only in the light of such an understanding can sense be made of Williams' poems' structures. For one is tempted, often, to talk about Williams' "metric," his measurement of the individual line, as distinct from his configuration for the whole poem, or even as something apart from groups of lines, what correspond to conventional stanzas.

Even Williams himself has done this at times, to the detriment of his intelligibility and effectiveness. But it simply cannot be done without doing violence to the poems as they really are. Neither, indeed, is it just or accurate to discuss the verse structures apart from the poems' language—the kinds of words Williams uses. Only the demands of making a manageable book make such a divorce perhaps a lesser evil than the overwhelming complicatedness of handling both at once. One must see that, perhaps unlike older verse forms, Williams' poems are "machines"—though "organisms" would seem a better term—composed of interrelated individual words, lines, groups of lines, all measured relative to each other and, ideally, each having value *only* in that relationship. Just as Williams has written *about* the problem of divorce in terms of images of wholeness or dissociation, he has made images of the reality of his world in the wholeness and brokenness of his poems' structures.

The function of "measure," whether the traditional poetic foot or a new unit such as Williams' "variable foot," is to free the mind—to draw the mind into its movement, which is the movement of the materials in the order of the poem, and away from the conventional movements (often only a stasis) of the mind's usual course. The measurement, the cadence—the "dance" into which the reader is drawn—liberates him to see the reltionships of the objects and, in a sense, liberates the objects from actuality's confusions, permitting them to be known more truly. We accept and—if the poem is good enough—make the poet's vision of reality a part of our own attitude toward the world. Nor is there a difference between line and over-all structure; what the arrangement of measured units accomplishes within the individual line is also accomplished by the various larger units in their arrangement as a whole poem.

This is not a new idea, certainly, yet it is all too often lost from sight in our discussions of literary works—even of the modern poem and even (or perhaps, especially) by the poets themselves, intent as they are upon what they have to "say." It is what Pound was reminding the reader of in his *ABC of Reading* when he remarked:

> The term "meaning" cannot be restricted to strictly intellectual or "coldly intellectual" significance. The how

much you mean it, the how you feel about meaning it, can all be "put into language." [1]

It was also what Williams found most impressive in James Joyce, something he pointed to in an editorial "Comment" in the first issue of *Contact*.

In the work of James Joyce the underlying fact which has impressed me is that by the form of his thought he has forced the reader into a new and special frame of mind favorable to the receipt of his disclosure. By his manner of putting down the words it is discovered that he is following some unapparent sequence quite apart from the usual syntactical one. [c28]

What Joyce did in—and for—the novel is what Williams has attempted to do in—and for—the poem: by his manner of putting down the words to cause the reader to find the unapparent and unusual sequence he is following.

Naturally, Williams' desire has caused him to experiment continually with ways of making poems, but essentially there have been three general modes, corresponding to three periods in his career: a period of apprenticeship in which—apparently at Pound's insistence—he turned from the conventional poetic modes of the earliest 1900's to newer (which then in some cases meant older) forms; a period from about the time of *Al Que Quiere* (1917) to the middle 1940's in which he explored and developed various techniques of his own; and, finally, the years after the publication of *Paterson IV*, during which time he seems to have settled pretty much on one scheme.

Of the three periods, the middle is both the most interesting and the most important to examine. The first is essentially a time when Williams was getting to know himself and the new ways of the poem, and his work from that period is now of little interest other than the historical. In his first book, *Poems* (1909), he wrote in what he says was the only form he then knew—rhymed couplets; in the second, *The Tempers*, he began to use his own manner and forms, but more often than not he employed those that Pound had been so brilliantly demonstrating. These latter poems are almost without exception his adaptations (by Pound's example) of old forms and subjects, frequently in rime, relying often upon

Poundian archaisms, and almost devoid of what Williams later called "the American idiom." Yet *The Tempers* does progress toward a more direct, more proselike, more flattened and precise statement (just as Pound himself progresses toward his *Cantos*), and there are three poems that do have more than merely antiquarian value: "To Mark Anthony in Heaven," "Le Médecin Malgré Lui," and "Portrait of a Lady." All use the language, structures, and materials that constituted his actual, and henceforth his poetic, world. And with his next book, *Al Que Quiere*, there was no longer any trace of the Elizabethan or the Provençal. Williams had discovered his poetic identity by rediscovering the world.

It is possible to say that the mode of work from *Al Que Quiere* on is based in imagism, but in saying only this one would be missing the fundamental value of Williams' verse. Anyone who has read anything about Williams knows of his association with the early imagists and of their influence not only upon him, but upon all of modern poetry. But Williams was never satisfied with imagism as a mode: in a talk at the University of Washington in 1948 he remarked that, "Imagism was not structural: that was the reason for its disappearance." [c283] It was not structural, or at least not in the sense of structure that involves the reflection of the nature of the poet's world in language. Yet it is equally evident that for Williams what has been of most importance in his structures has been the clear, precise image as the fundamental unit, the building block. It has not been the line as a unit of measurement, a collection of so many stresses, or feet, but the sense-unit, and as one corollary of his belief in "no ideas but in things," that unit has had to be the image. In this sense, each image is one relatively complex "thing" capable of containing within it an idea.

Williams' experimentation, therefore, has been in two intimately connected areas: what constitutes an image, and how one may put images together to form a poem. Ideally, of course, if one could make an image identical with a line, one would have an excellent start toward a new form—or forms—that might be varied and yet maintained, as the sonnet was. But unless one assumes the image to be far simpler than it obviously is, this leads to the sort of loose, seemingly endless, unmeasurable line

that one finds in the worst of Whitman—precisely the
sort of writing that Williams was attempting to avoid.
The obvious alternative is to break the image into its
parts, like breaking a molecule of vision into its atoms, the
irreducible pieces of communicative matter. And this is
the method that occupied Williams' attentions.

A wonderful example of how such pieces may be
variously conceived and arranged occurs in the comparison of the two versions of "Sparrows Among Dry Leaves."
In the earlier of the two, Williams was obviously interested in creating the clearest possible images of the things
in the poem *as things*.

> *The sparrows*
> *by the iron fence-post*
> *hardly seen*
>
> *for the dry leaves*
> *that half*
> *cover them—*
>
> *stirring up*
> *the leaves—fight*
> *and chirp*
>
> *stridently*
> *search*
> *and*
>
> *peck the sharp*
> *gravel to*
> *good digestion*
>
> *and love's*
> *obscure and insatiable*
> *appetite* [a458]

In the later version the poem is arranged into lines that
carry more complex sense units.

> *The sparrows by the iron fence post—*
> *hardly seen for the dry leaves*
> *that half cover them—*
> *stirring up the leaves, fight*
> *and chirp stridently, search and*
> *peck the sharp gravel to*
> *good digestion and love's*
> *obscure and insatiable appetite.* [b55]

Here is a fascinating view of the process of experimentation. Although the individual objects and actions are far more sharply defined in the first poem, the movement of that version is too slow, there are too many separate things, as in the actual world: the poem has the shape of actuality, but not the implication of the shape of reality that is carried within the organization of the second version. The first is undoubtedly the more striking of the two. The clarity, the sharpness of its focus upon the common things and actions, magnifies each and gives it an importance, an immediacy that forces it upon our attention as it would not come to our notice in the everyday world; each piece (line) bursts upon us with an energy that the other arrangement cannot achieve. Yet the poem is defective, as Williams himself seems to have felt, in its failure to convey an image of the connectedness of the pieces.

The second version attempts to make each line an image of relationships; each line connects the sparrows to something nominally outside them. Just as the poem is concerned with the underlying unity of all life seen in terms of love as both a function and a corollary of normal life in the natural world—the sparrows becoming representative of love's vitality, its satisfactions, and yet its ambivalence—so the poem's structure is an image of this oneness. Where the earlier structure reflected the apparent uniquenesses of the actual, here is imaged the vision of the real behind the unique's seeming separations.

What each line in the later version amounts to is a sense-unit, an image not only of what, but how, while in the earlier poem the unit is each three-line section. Apparently, however, Williams' idea of *precisely* what constituted the unit changed in the rewriting; there is not an exact correspondence between each three-line element and its counterpart line later. Nor is each unit "perfect" in the second poem, though the previous version attempts the complete unity of each image; with the longer line and its attempt at establishing relationships Williams adds carryover words at the ends of some lines in order to begin the images of the following units and further reflect the connectedness of all in the poem.

Although these nonidentical twin poems are short, they serve admirably as evidences of the foundations of Williams' structural method and at the same time of the difficulties it has created, both for Williams as maker and for the reader attempting to know what Williams is about. For it is clear from even a quick glance at his poems that Williams has not felt constrained to use conventional syntactical patterns any more than he has seen a need for conventional poetic forms. Williams has tried to leave out the words that ordinarily indicate the general relationships of one group of words to another, and has attempted, instead, to pack each poem with the greatest possible number of objective images. Again no ideas but in things. In "Sparrows Among Dry Leaves" the syntax is normal, but the words such as "and" and "by" are almost redundant; the relationships of sparrow to fence, of fighting to chirping, and of searching to pecking are indicated by the simple juxtaposition of image to image, sense-unit to sense-unit. The poem progresses not by any logical, rational means, but by the process of accretion. One thing is added to another in such fashion that its mere proximity creates a connection that modifies both by making them relative to each other. In a sense, Williams' juxtaposed identifications perform the same function that conventional metaphor accomplishes with usually less complex units, and we see previously unperceived relationships.

This accretive method is the basic means that Williams has employed ever since *Al Que Quiere*. Whatever else he has done in making a poem, Williams has done it with images, units of idea and (in) object, built one upon another like the layers of a pearl deposited (often unevenly) upon a center of irritation. In this he is at the center of modern artistic practice, expressing a (for him) broken world, a world without logical connections, without overt or perceptible connections of any sort, expressing, perhaps, the irrational consciousness of man, producing, like Joyce, like the cubist painters, a view of the world not from only one point but from many.

At its most extreme, the accretive technique pieces together fragments—broken reflections of the actual world. In the longer poems—poems of, say, more than a page—where Williams has the opportunity to work with a large enough number of pieces, even this incompleteness of the image is not necessarily in itself disturbing or destructive; as in a large mosaic picture, a fine Byzantine, perhaps, the individual pieces lose their identities, and the emergence of the whole picture, the complex of relationships, is all that occupies the mind. Yet often the fragments are too raw, too actual, too unassimilated to the totality of the poem. In "Della Primavera Trasportata Al Morale," an early long poem, one finds examples of the sorts of fragmented images Williams was to use with varying success in several later poems. Concerned with the actual sights and sounds about him, Williams juxtaposes them with fragmentary comments just as he juxtaposes elements of the natural world with elements of the human and its constructs. Beginning with a section of continuous development, Williams establishes his base in the natural continuity of seasonal change:

APRIL

> *the beginning—or*
> *what you will:*
> > *the dress*
> *in which the veritable winter*
> *walks in Spring—*
>
> *Loose it!*
> *Let it fall (where it will)*
> *—again* [a57]

From the following images of flowers, however, Williams moves abruptly to a series of fragments seemingly opposed to both the wholeness and the beauty of the natural, coming to a series of lists of different kinds through an indented interpolation:

> *a green truck*
> *dragging a concrete mixer*
> *passes*
> *in the street—*
> *the clatter and true sound.*
> *of verse—* [a59]

This section works perfectly in the poem; because the materials of both terms of the metaphor are made by men, they establish a basic connection upon which to build the identity Williams sees—the typical reflections of the modern world—and the fragment formally establishes the relationship between the disparate elements of the poem.

The first of the poem's lists follows an image of the natural world. Juxtaposed to "—the wind is howling / the river, shining mud—" is a series of items each introduced by the word "Moral," each item offering a fragment of either subjective feeling or objective description. All this culminates in "—the moral is love, bred of / the mind and eyes and hands—" There ensues a section of consecutive statement in a normal logical progression that is broken, finally, by "STOP : STOP," followed in turn by another list, each item beginning with "I believe," the section ending in

THIS IS MY PLATFORM

I believe in your love

the first dandelion
flower at the edge of—[a61]

Another series of juxtaposed fragments follows, coupling the opposed themes of the natural world (flowers and love) and the prosaic details of everyday modern life, and returning periodically to "I believe." The whole central section of the poem culminates in the completely undigested details of:

I believe
Spumoni	$1.00
French Vanilla	.70
Chocolate	.70
Strawberry	.70
Maple Walnut	.70
Coffee	.70
Tutti Frutti	.70
Pistachio	.70
Cherry Special	.70
Orange Ice	.70
Biscuit Tortoni	

25¢ per portion

trees—seeming dead:
    the long years—

tactus eruditus

Maple, I see you have
a squirrel in your crotch—

and you have a woodpecker
in your hole, Sycamore

—a fat blonde, in purple (no trucking
on this street)

POISON!

[skull and cross bones]

I believe

WOMAN'S WARD

[directional arrow, left]

PRIVATE

[directional arrow, right]

The soul, my God, shall rise up
—a tree [a62–63]

Williams' intent is apparently to fuse these diverse elements of the major portion of his poem, and to stimulate the reader's understanding of their relationships, by his concluding section, especially in

The forms
of the emotions are crystalline,
geometric-faceted. So we recognize
only in the white heat of
understanding, when a flame
runs through the gap made
by learning, the shapes of things—
the ovoid sun, the pointed trees [a64]

This is the return to the idea that has appeared fragmentarily in the conclusions to the two previous lists, and it is clearly a statement not only of what he has "to say," but of how he has been proving his "meaning" in his structure.

Unfortunately, in this poem his method does not work well: the poem does not get sufficiently behind the shapes of actuality, it does not pierce through to the real. Going from the natural world to the pieces of the human, Williams fails to establish clear enough points of contact between the two realms; only his repeated return to April-flowers-love offers any point of entry to the poem's broken world. And the movement from list to list tells the reader too little. The first list builds upon the distortion of "moral"; expecting the abstract generalization that the word ordinarily denotes, the reader gets instead a series of personal, specific, and increasingly concrete disconnected fragments. True judgments, one sees, are not conventionally universal—and therefore removed from the individual man—but a series of personal experiences that add up to "love, bred of / the mind and eyes and hands—" that is, a unique intimate relationship between a man and his world created and maintained through the particulars that form his life.

The second list reverses the sort of expectation, but it uses the same sort of distortion: expecting a series of sincere personal beliefs, one gets only a list of conventional political campaign declarations, the meaningless language of the public man, running on into the mechanical repetition of "I believe." The culmination of the list is Williams' reversion to the real, "I believe in your love"; contrasting with the insincerity of the previous beliefs, this offers a truth, again personal. Here "belief" is the proper word: love must be believed in, since it cannot be objectively proved, and love (as the means to men's wholeness through intimate contact) is the foundation of Williams' attitude in the poem. Ultimately Williams returns to the declaration of beliefs, but uses a new kind of material believed in:

> I believe
>> Moving to three doors
>> above—May 1st.
>
> I believe
>> ICE—and warehouse site [a62]

This is his transition to the reflection of the other side of the modern mind—its belief in the world actually about it, the things at the very surface of modern life. But these things are also what Williams does believe in, at least in one sense, for he does believe that this is *his* world, what his poems must reflect. And so he comes finally to the ostensibly ironic ice cream menu as his belief. Here is actuality reproduced photographically—to be followed by the reproductions of the three labels, the three images, one must guess, of communication in our time—communication weakened, cheapened, mass produced and depersonalized.

Such an analysis of the poem is fine, if true. But the really serious defect of the poem is that even if it is true, one ought not have to piece it together; by Williams' own standards one ought to see the poem as a work of the imagination. Yet such elements as the list of ice creams are accretions of raw data, unrefined by the imagination; they are chance accumulations rather than orders of reality suddenly made apparent in the everyday things of our lives. This poem is still a series of improvisations, very much like his book of "prose" improvisations, *Kora in Hell*; and it has the same fault. In both, the exercises in the imagination lack a *perceptible* structure; while the mind can go from one thing to another without apparent plan, art, as Williams says, cannot—it is *made*, it is deliberate. The improvisations are thus too unformed to be fully expressive of their intent; even the different kinds of interpretations that Williams inserts in the two works are not enough to form the works. They have too much the appearance of merely by chance having become what they are. At best they copy nature, not imitate it.

Yet when Williams is at his best in the long poems, he is able to present materials in the state closest to the way we find them in our daily lives and yet transform them. In an essay on Pound's *Cantos* in 1931 Williams spoke of "the principal move in imaginative writing today—that away from the word as symbol toward the word as reality." [c107] Somewhat later in the essay, having spoken of the rhythm (or movement) of the poem as the movement of the poet's thought, "as the movement of a horse becomes a part of the rider also," [c108] he goes on to say:

> It is in the minutiae—in the minute organization of the words and their relationships in a composition that the seriousness and value of a work of writing exist—*not* in the sentiments, ideas, schemes portrayed.
> It is here, furthermore, that creation takes place. It is not a plaster of thought applied.
> The seriousness of a work of art, the belief the author has in it, is that he does generate in it—a solution in some sense of the continuous confusion and barrenness which life imposes in its mutations—(on him who will not create). [c109]

Thus it is that "the movement of his mind" can include

not only the acknowledged beauties of the world, but such seemingly unpoetic matters as the list of groceries in the poem about his ailing ninety-year-old grandmother entitled "Two Pendants: for the Ears." The title is more than a mere decoration or catchphrase; it indicates that this poem is mainly aural—it is conversation with his grandmother, to whom he must talk; conversation with those sitting sick watch with her; reportings of things she is supposed to have said. And in the midst of this talk Williams places:

> Listen, I said, I met a man
> last night told me what he'd brought
> home from the market:
>   2 partridges
>   2 Mallard ducks
>   a Dungeness crab
>   24 hours out
>   of the Pacific
>   and 2 live-frozen
>   trout
>   from Denmark [b221–22]

Into the stream of dull, prosaic conversation Williams brings what should by normal standards be more of the same, but turns out to be about exotic things; he sets up a counterpoint of expectation and result. Thus one movement of his thought. But the movement takes another strange turn; the list of (unusual) groceries turns out to be not so much an ordinary list as another way of measuring things—which is, after all, what any list does really, though we don't ordinarily think of it in that sense. After the first three items, each commencing with a number, Williams places another number that is not a measure of kind, but presumably, first, of time and, second, of place, which two qualifications comprise, finally, what amounts to enough restriction of the crab's qualities to become still another measure of kind. (The restriction of qualities makes *this* crab different from other Dungeness crabs.) In this way, when one arrives at the last item, "and 2 live-frozen/trout/from Denmark," one unconsciously presupposes the same sort of structure and sees each line as a unit of measurement of the nature of the whole, more complex thing, which is precisely the "new order" that Williams aims at. His apparently unnecessary breaking of the item into three lines serves the purpose of reestablishing the words' vitality; they serve not as symbols for something else outside the poem, but as a new reality within the poem. The familiar combination of words becomes not something seen on a package of food, but a new combination of three units of measurement of a part of our world whose complexity we fail to notice.

This use of the line as a unit of measurement underlies most of Williams' work. The poem "Blueflags" is a good example of how this accretion of sense-units can be carried out without the breaks in thought, without the sudden shifts of mind among seemingly unrelated images.

> I stopped the car
> to let the children down
> where the streets end
> in the sun
> at the marsh edge
> and the reeds begin
> and there are small houses
> facing the reeds
> and the blue mist
> in the distance
> with grapevine trellises
> with grape clusters
> small as strawberries
> on the vines
> and ditches
> running springwater
> that continue the gutters
> with willows over them.
> The reeds begin
> like water at a shore
> their petals waving
> dark green and light.
> But blueflags are blossoming
> in the reeds
> which the children pluck
> chattering in the reeds
> high over their heads
> which they part
> with bare arms to appear
> with fists of flowers
> till in the air
> there comes the smell
> of calamus
> from wet, gummy stalks. [a225]

Here the movement of Williams' mind is the process of simple additions; each line adds a new detail to the picture. The poem is a sort of set-piece, in some ways seemingly an impossible topic to handle without falling into sentimentality and blur. Yet Williams handles his material in such fashion that he descends to neither; he maintains clarity by using the smallest possible units and, where possible, by breaking the line at the point where the reader knows what the image contains but not why it is there. Thus in the first three lines, for instance, one is given first the action, then the reason for it, and finally the reason for that mediate cause—that is, one realizes that the nature of the place is the cause for the children's getting out of the car.

If one were to object that this constant accretion of word to word and understanding to understanding is what language *always* does, the only answer would be that, certainly, it does, but. . . . In poems like "Blueflags" the formal arrangement prevents the reader from making the assumptions that ordinarily support his understanding; while within each line the words are directly related to each other in a normal syntactical arrangement, and in fact a word in one line is normally related to a word or group of words in another, each line also forms a self-sustaining piece that has its own relationship to the fragment preceding it and the fragment following. Nor are these relationships indicated by the usual signs of cause and effect. Only by building in the mind an imaginative recreation of the structure of the poem's world can the reader grasp *for himself* the "meaning" of the poem.

It is unfortunate, even unjust, but unavoidable not to be able to reproduce in full one of Williams' better poems to demonstrate what happens when Williams' method works at its best. But if "Della Primavera Trasportata Al Morale" is too broken and too much merely unformed actuality, and if "Blueflags" is too slight, the wonderful "An Elegy for D. H. Lawrence" succeeds by its juxtapositions of pieces in creating an imaginative continuity that evokes both Williams' state of mind as he thinks of Lawrence and the essence of Lawrence as a man and as an artist.

There is no question of finding in this poem a precise,

symmetrical structure; the stanzas are irregular, the lines
more so, and the themes and materials of the poem are
not set in any exactly measurable order. Yet, clearly,
Williams has cut the pieces of his mosaic according to a
plan. For one thing, while he establishes a continuity with
the repetitions and variations of the themes of spring-and-
summer, the qualities of place (England as opposed to the
hot places of Lawrence's "exile"), the symbolic serpent,
and human contact by talk, at the same time he carefully
separates the stanzas so that each is a distinct entity.
There are none of the conventional connectives to link
one with another, no developing narrative or other framework of chronological continuity, no premises and conclusions. There is instead an expansion of Williams' first
statement, his placing together in one seemingly coinci-
dental coupling of the budding shrub and Lawrence dead.
This is the unit of idea that he maintains throughout.
Used in any ordinary way, such a would-be paradox of the
world's coming into renewed life with Lawrence's death
would be trite at best, a pat image for a common idea; but
Williams avoids any direct involvement with the intellectual attractions of paradox as such and goes ahead to
create his identification of Lawrence with the same life
that draws the green from within the stem. By opposing
this energy, this "April's promise," to the stillness, the
deadness of the older culture, the older world—the
"Ashes / of Cretan fires"—Williams finally establishes a
finer irony than exists in the simple life-from-death
convention: Lawrence is finally *the* representative of the
English genius, the human equivalent of the temperate
lands' flowers, "passed unwanted" in (and from) the very
time and place whose qualities he enlarges and purifies.

The unstated quality of spring that here unifies all
Williams' materials—and distinguishes them from the
materials of his older world—is its fertility, its sexuality.
And it is through this quality that Williams involves
Lawrence in the poem through his writing. Lawrence's
promise is contained in his sexuality, the very quality that
England rejected, both in his life and in his work, and this
spirit is represented by the convention of the serpent—a
Laurentian symbol as well—who *becomes* Lawrence just
as do the flowers. The serpent is always presented juxtaposed to an image of the natural world, flowers usually,

until the multiple identity is secure. In effect, Williams has done for Lawrence what Lawrence wished to do: he has represented the natural world's oneness in sexuality, ending with the cricket's sad sound where the snake-Lawrence-sexuality has disappeared.

The structure of the poem is effective. Without recourse to either a conventional order of reasoning or a conventional measurement of his poetic construction, Williams manages to communicate both his ideas and his feelings in a memorable way. By the simple process of placing image against image, he causes the reader to bridge the gaps with his own understanding. But Williams here works out his progression carefully, so that what is at the beginning only a reflection of actuality's appearances becomes at the last an image of what really is: the more Williams adds bits from the surface of what happened, the more one sees the truth of what was. In part this is because he has chosen things that have naturally some quality in common with what he wishes to represent; except for the serpent, none of his materials is an arbitrary symbol. Even the snake itself has, as psychological symbol, commonly accepted sexual qualities—and certainly his image of the snake in the pool and the water dripping from the rock is a clear physical representation of the sexual act. But in part, too, the clarity of the poem derives from Williams' sparing but efficient use of words and phrases that lead the reader to look for the proper "meanings." His use of "*poor* Lawrence," for instance, turns the reader's mind toward an attitude; his insertion of such comment as "and it grows clearer / what bitterness drove him" makes Williams' intent clearer, too. The poem is not constituted merely of objectified images, precise pictures of the world, removed from the poet; the poet's attitudes toward that world are indicated quite precisely.

Unfortunately, in the short poems, which make up the greatest part of his work and for which he is still best known, Williams fails at time to make successful structures because he uses a fragment of actuality not only to make a poem of, but as a means of building toward a new poetic convention. In his unsureness of his readers' responses toward his materials, he often feels called upon to reconstruct actuality from the beginning, to take it in its absolutely raw state—as he finds it about him—and by assimilating it gradually to the development of the poem, show the process of transforming it into an imaginative order. In the long poem this can be effective, but in the short work it is an impossible task; if he is not to end with too much material for too little (discernible) order, he must transform and order the materials before he presents them in the poem. Yet if he does complete this process before writing, he must rely upon implication far more than the conventional poet does; his materials from the actual world must come to the underlying reality by an extreme process of indirection.

By looking at an unsuccessful poem or two, one can perhaps see best how the successes are achieved. In "The Stylist," written in the late forties, when Williams had long since been extremely successful in this vein, he reverts to the "slice of life"—or perhaps more properly chunk of life, ripped as it is from the fabric of the actions of everyday life.

> Long time no see.
> —*a flash as*
> *from polished steel,*
> *then:*
>
> *I've been too*
> *damned poor to get out*
> *of the woods. I was*
> *expecting you*
> *to come up and bring*
> *me into town.*
>
> *No answer.* [b110]

As a perception and reproduction of an action, and even of a minute part of the second speaker's character, the poem is accurate, even brilliant, in its precision and brevity. Its structure is perfectly worked out to make each line end at such a point that the reader sees the next as an addition to his understanding of the growing view; each line could, in fact, have any number of possible alternative additions that would differ widely in their explanations of what happened and why it happened—as, for instance, "to get out" might conclude "of town," "of the house," "of debt," and so forth. But for all its cleverness, for all its artistic intelligence, the poem does not, to use

Williams' own standard, convey any "useful knowledge." Even if it is meant—if any poem can be meant—to be purely reportorial, it reports too few facts. But if it is meant (as I believe) to give a perception of the underlying reality of the world and our personal relationships, it doesn't pierce deeply enough into the structure of motives and actions, of causes and effects. It is *too* indirect.

In "Sour Grapes" the poem "The Great Figure" appeared, and it was singled out subsequently for reprinting and favorable comment. Yet it, too, is an image of experience reproduced *too* literally; the experience has not been enough *made* as a poem.

> Among the rain
> and lights
> I saw the figure 5
> in gold
> on a red
> firetruck
> moving
> tense
> unheeded
> to gong clangs
> siren howls
> and wheels rumbling
> through the dark city. [a230]

As a significant structure this is somewhat more successful than "The Stylist," first, because Williams has the opportunity to compose the various physical elements into a sort of sensual (perceptual) order and, second, because the words "moving / tense / unheeded" give to the fire engine a start toward relationship with its immediate world. Still, the indirection is too great; one sees too little of either the world or the poet. When one finishes he has little more than a visual image drawn with marvelous skill, and Williams has not supplied him with matter in such form that he is richer in understanding—or even mere acceptance—of the world. The figure 5 fails to gain importance by extensions of implication—even an irrational, purely emotional sudden importance in the poet's mind, which would tell the reader something about the nature of men. This irrationality *seems* to be the center of the poem, but again the structure is too indirect to hold such unrefined materials.

What such poems lack is some specified point of

relation to the rest of the world, such as the statement that makes "The Red Wheelbarrow" so successful; "so much depends" creates the conceptual structure for the whole poem and gives the reader a focus upon the things of that poetic world. The poem "Between Walls" establishes a structure by presenting a different kind of condition, only an indirect statement—the state of the world in which the poem's elements exist (see p. 46). The clarity of meaning here is remarkable for such a lean, spare poem with such an implicit idea. It has been made possible, first, by the structure of similarities and individual differences; second, by the comparison and contrast of the natural and made worlds; and, finally, by the implication of the human as cause of the conditions and as the percipient of the facts and their relationships. The words "where / nothing / will grow" are the agents of ramification here. To begin with, they indicate the implied difference of appearance between the deadness of the cinders and the shine of the glass; the pieces of bottle become, in the poet's mind, a substitute for the vegetation that will not grow. What attracts the poet is the appearance or illusion of what he knows cannot be, and he perceives beauty shining forth in the midst of drabness, as one must always find it; his action is the classic esthetic act. But also implied is the original agency of the barrenness of the place: men have made the building and put down the cinders, thus forming a mechanical-construct seemingly cut off from the natural world. Suddenly, however, this mechanical world evidences a parallel to the natural, through the imagination. In addition there is the implied parallel between the refuse-cinders (burnt-out and discarded) and the refuse-bottle (emptied and discarded), but this becomes in the poem's structure a dissimilarity as the broken glass greenly becomes identified instead with the also discarded, unwanted grass. The poem includes, therefore, two opposed qualities of the human mind—the rational, practical, wasteful, destructive part that builds *vs.* the imaginative, perceptive, conservative, ordering part that creates; a series of causes and effects that derive from those qualities of mind; and the points of divergence and the points of congruence of the human, natural, and mechanical-construct worlds. In the indirection of the poem as we see it all this is only implicit, yet it is available.

Something more than merely a comment should be made about the relationship between Williams' poems and modern painting, for in their similarities there lie further indications of Williams' modes of structure. That the similarities are deliberate and not merely products of a general artistic spirit of a period is to be seen in the perhaps external but none the less valid facts of Williams' youthful uncertainty about whether to become a painter or a poet, his continuing interest in painting, and the many painters among his friends—Sheeler, Demuth, Hartley, and others. That the similarities do actually exist is demonstrable in an examination of any number of his poems; and in fact his friend Charles Demuth transformed "The Great Figure" into a painting by translating the verbal images into visual and retaining the multiplicity of broken images, superimposed upon one another at some points, placed against each other at others.

The truth is that Williams' work is often the product of the painter's eye and the painter's methods; the imagistic, the fragmented collocations of individual small "pictures" is the literary counterpart to modern painting's cubism— the attempt to show things not as they seem, the apparent "wholes" being but illusions, but recomposed of their various parts, their various shapes, in such fashion that their reality, if not any longer their full actuality, is perceptible. This concept may account for much of Williams' work being completely free from interpretation or comment—the images stand alone, the things in themselves, with only the method of their arrangement to give (implicitly) any understanding of their "meaning" (reality). Just as the painters dropped spatial perspective as the basis for their relationships, Williams dropped the "perspective" of temporal and syntactical (causal) relationships. (Thus, too, as Picasso can employ a flat primitive mode as true now, Williams can use "primitive" modes in *Paterson* or can believe that the Greek "exists now in Preakness.") Such is the case, apparently, with "Spring and All." Published originally with prose sections alternated with the numbered (but untitled) poem sections, it has been stripped even further in the collected works by the omission of the prose. Thus the *whole* poem —so infrequently regarded as a whole—is composed of the twenty-eight individual poems, each a separable piece, it is true, but each gaining in significance by its relationship to the general context. And each individual poem, in turn, becomes a picture, a clearly outlined view of the subject (now primarily *object*) with the emphasis on the visual "effect" upon the perceiver; Williams puts the poem together by assembling the various aspects of the subject (object) in the manner of the cubists: it is composed of pieces, few complete, but each clear insofar as it goes. For instance, "The Pot of Flowers":

> Pink confused with white
> flowers and flowers reversed
> take and spill the shaded flame
> darting it back
> into the lamp's horn
>
> petals aslant darkened with mauve
>
> red where in whorls
> petal lays its glow upon petal
> round flamegreen throats
>
> petals radiant with transpiercing light
> contending
>   above
> the leaves
> reaching up their modest green
> from the pot's rim
>
> and there, wholly dark, the pot
> gay with rough moss. [a242]

Beginning with the topmost portion of the object he views—the part most immediate to the viewer's notice— Williams works downward to the plant's base in the pot; he builds from the bright colors to the dark, from the confusion of petalled brilliance to the relative simplicity of the moss. Word-counts probably prove nothing ordinarily, but it is nonetheless interesting to note that of the sixty-seven words in the poem twelve are either the names of colors or descriptions of light, and ten more are the names of things that possess color or give light; one third of the poem, in short, is the direct presentation of light and color. The poem's effect upon the reader is therefore one of the movement of color-masses; from the beginning in the first line's mixing of pink and white as abstracted qualities, the poem moves in line-images that each offer a different, fragmented view of the interplay between colors and between the light's true source and its seeming regeneration in the flowers' brilliance, until the unmoving "modest green" and the pot's indeterminate darkness hold as the centrum of the structure.

Any number of other poems from "Spring and All" would serve similar analyses: "Flight to the City," in its extreme fragmentation; "The Rose," with its various kinds of rose figure—the different senses of the word superimposed upon each other; "At the faucet of June," its wild leaps among disparate objects like the use of scraps of actuality in a collage; in fact, virtually any poem in the collection. Nor is "Spring and All" the only source for evidence; Williams' deservedly praised clarity of detail, his sense of the thing as thing in all its distinctness, is constant evidence of his poems' kinship to painting.

The inevitable final result of a technique, like Williams', that attempts to construct poems out of pieces of actuality is that it works always toward compression, toward the stripping away of all words but the absolutely indispensable denotations of the objects; it relies less than conventional verse upon particles, intensifiers, qualifiers, all the words that regulate the shades of meaning by talking *about* the objects. If this leads, perhaps, to less subtlety in expression of intellectual materials, it does certainly lead to great energy being pent up in the poem. The two versions of "The Locust Tree in Flower" exemplify how the stripping achieves such energy. Here Williams almost achieves what his work is always moving toward: the ultimate compression in which everything—every word, every sound, almost—is so fertile with implication that it must burst from the confines of strictest meanings and loose the half-hidden-half-felt threads of a radiating web of associations and extended meanings. This is of course what all poets seek; Williams is not unique in this. His contribution here is the reduction of the line to the single word. The (for Williams, at least) conventional units of structure, the line and the word, becoming identical, but the reader *expecting* more from the line than he gets, the unit leaves a vacuum, intellectual as well as emotional, that the reader *must* fill from the associations, the connotations, that inevitably a poem frees but too often the reader forces back into the darkness of the mind. The differences between the earlier and later versions and between one's reactions to them are evident.

(first version)

Among
the leaves
bright

green
of wrist-thick
tree

and old
stiff broken
branch

ferncool
swaying
loosely strung—

come May
again
white blossom

clusters
hide
to spill

their sweets
almost
unnoticed

down
and quickly
fall [a94]

(second version)

Among
of
green

stiff
old
bright

broken
branch
come

white
sweet
May

again [a93]

Though more obviously in the second version, both of these depend to a great extent upon the convention of the line containing more than one word and more than one accented syllable—except, of course, in the cases of lines deliberately shortened for emphasis by their difference from the rest of the poem. As a result of the reader's conditioning he tends to expect more than he gets, and he is forced to seek out the implied ramifications—both logical (denotative) and associational (connotative)—of the framework—in effect to flesh out the skeleton. But there is also here the feeling of the material working to break the restrictions of the form—as there should be in any poem. The conflict between this expansive tendency of words and the restrictive nature of the poem's structure, here in the maximum possible opposition, creates the underlying energy and excitement that is the initial emotional charge in the poem. For whatever else one may hold in his esthetic, he cannot escape the fact that in any poem the primary pleasure is born of the audience's immediate realization of the poem's artifice and their appreciation, first, of the difficulty of making the artifice contain a life of its own; second, of using materials (words) not created especially and specifically for that artifice (or artifact); and finally, of the poem's maintaining a conflict between art and nature in which both are heightened and supported by each other and neither is victorious at the other's expense. Perhaps this is as much as to say that one's *first* pleasure in a poem is intellectual rather than emotional, since if one does not realize the fact of the poem's artifice—that is, its existence *as a poem*, a thing made, an entity with a nature of its own—he cannot enjoy or understand it *as a poem* although he may applaud its sentiments or ideas, be unknowingly moved by its sound, or in some other way react to it partially. But he cannot speak, or even think, of the poem as a whole. It is the knowledge of the poem as art, *as a poem*, that creates not only a pleasure of its own, but the conditions for a complete enjoyment of all that is available.

This is not a question of mere admiration for mental gymnastics, though that can become a factor—especially in the presence of metaphysical conceits or exceptionally intricate rhyme scheme or metric—but a matter of the reader's understanding of what is being done and how it is accomplished. One of the major reasons for photography's inability to equal painting in artistic importance is this inequality, in a photograph, between nature and art: the thing represented is always essentially in its actual natural state; whatever the photographer's imagination, the means of his art are insufficient to create the intensity of conflict between what is there and what he imagines that is necessary for major art. Photographically, a rose *is* a rose is a rose.

In the case of "The Locust Tree in Flower" this opposition between nature and art is what leads to the perceptions of the significance of Williams' materials. In both versions of the poem—though considerably more so in the later—the composition of the selected materials is what strikes the reader. These are poems to be seen, not merely to be heard. But in the first poem Williams tells one more than the facts warrant; for all its strippedness it contains redundancies. "Wrist-thick," for instance, adds nothing that goes further than what it says denotatively; "old / stiff broken" present qualities that describe the tree's uniqueness at the same time as they place it in a whole class of similar objects, but "wrist-thick" is both too specific and too limited—perhaps too accidental—to offer any useful knowledge about the way in which this tree is significant. In the same way, the last twelve lines present information that is at once too unique and too restrictive to say much more than Williams tells us. Because the lines are abbreviated, one senses that there ought to be more there than he perceives immediately; but because Williams tells him so much, he can see only the image of a specific isolated case.

In the second version, however, the stripping is marvelously effective. Upon first reading the poem, one is inclined to suppose that it is composed of almost nothing but nouns and verbs, of solidities and action; yet only two words are nouns—and one of them the name of a month—just one a verb. The impression of solidity, of things, derives from the isolation of words ordinarily hidden in the welter of a sentence. Finding the word "Among" immediately unrelated syntactically to anything but "of" —which structure makes no sense logically—the reader is forced to hold in his mind the general meaning of the word while he goes on in the poem. But "among" implies plurality, usually of concrete objects, so that one must assume the poem's field filled with things. From this idea of the distributive, one moves to the idea of the collective, the possessive, a sort of identification, in the second unit, "of." Thus if the two words do not make logical sense, they certainly make an impressionistic sort of poetic sense, especially because one must give his mind to pure concept, relationships left blank, to be filled in further on. "Green" in the next line completes the first three-line sense-unit with another dissociated quality; while conceivably the word might be used as a simple conventional modifier, it takes on a half-life of its own here, implying some possessor(s) of greenness. But "green" supplies the objective reference for the first two lines, and one finally fills out the double image of being within the green to the extent of becoming— or feeling—identified with it.

The second three-line sense-unit is built in exactly the same fashion as the first, except that the reference for the adjectives is withheld. That is, each line implies a possessor of its quality, and lacking the name of that possessor, one holds the *idea* of physical things concurrently with the idea of stiffness, oldness, and brightness. Yet if the—ness form of the word to indicate the abstraction would be weak, static, the generalization in the mind from the stated qualities is not; rather, the unit gains strength from the mind's having to perform the same kind of process of abstraction and re-formation into actual existence with which it is constantly involved in dealing with the world around it. In fact, the object(s)—as yet still undetermined—is known finally *only* by those qualities; they become the representation of the object, become a new kind of solidity.

The third sense-unit is the pivot about which the understanding swings; here is supplied the specific thing

and the action, and the previous, generalized understanding of the poem takes a restricted focus. The new
interpretation is ambivalent, however, since one cannot
simply dismiss from his mind the order of generalized
possibility he has constructed, nor does the addition of
"branch" diminish the idea of the previously mentioned
qualities existing as the physical object. All that happens
is that the branch is the specific thing that becomes these
qualities. The reader's mind thus works in two directions
at once; toward the concrete, the specific, the restricted—
the branch; and toward the abstract, the general, the
inclusive—the world, which the branch comes to represent. This duality is a repetition of the combination of the
distributive and the collective in the first unit, since
distribution implies particularity and collectiveness implies generalization. But at this point the form of the verb
brings in a new disagreement: "come" does not agree with
"branch," and causes the reader to accept not only an
indeterminate subject but the possibility that the verb
may be in one or another of various modes, tenses, and
numbers. Further than this, the indeterminateness of
"come" serves to express the inherent oneness of the elements of the poem, the impossibility of separating the
terms before "come" from the terms after: it is connected
formally to "branch" as intimately as it is syntactically to
the following subject.

In beginning with "white" the fourth sense-unit offers a
possible subject, if one takes whiteness as the same sort of
generalized solidity that "green" was. By considering this
possibility, the reader magnifies the term, and while he
later realizes that the specific reference of the word is to
flowers—just as the green is the leaves—he makes the
quality equivalent to the thing, May, and interchangeable
with it, which is precisely what the poem has done in his
own mind. The poem thus fills out all its lacunae and
forms a whole image of wholeness, of the interconnected-
ness of leaf, branch, flower, color, smell, time. Even
without the last word it would stand of its own solidity.
But the last line qualifies the entire structure by its
implication of evanescence, of all these elements having
once been fused, then separated, as they will be again. It
adds, in other words, another kind of unity, the oneness of
past, present, and future. This is the echo of the desire

and implication in the exhortation "come"; the structure is one not merely of acceptance of the fact of the present, but of hope and desire for what will grow from it.

There is one further aspect of the poem's structure that ought to be remarked—its appearance on the page. For the starkness of the poem is a reflection of the bareness of the tree; at the same time, the words' pregnancy with implication and their effect of beauty are the equivalent of the beauty and promise of the flowers. Carried within the stripped poem are the same possibilities as those carried within the stripped tree. Perhaps the poem and the tree, too, become finally interchangeable.

It could be misleading to offer the two versions of "The Locust Tree in Flower" as the first representative examples of Williams' way of paring down his poems; especially would it be misleading to make them appear typical in the degree of their strippedness. But they *are* typical in that they are the paradigm of his method, the manner purified and representative of *all* the cleanliness and compression of his work. In one degree or another, therefore, each poem is compressed, the words pruned to the greatest possible economy by squeezing the ideas back into the materials rather than drawing them out into explicit statement. Not only the early work is stripped, but the later, too; not only the extremely short line but the fuller, longer line; not only the poem of the brief, quick glance, but the poem of greater scope, up to and including "Paterson." Especially, this is the technique of the poems written during the great depression or in some way conditioned by it; so often, in them, Williams presents a slice of life cut cleanly away from the matrix in which it has been formed, as if to indicate that life is too hard to bear except in slices or too broken for the perception of more than a piece at a time. In poems like "The RR Bums" (see p. 95), for instance, he holds up a bit of the modern world stripped to a skeletal existence. Less purely "objective" than "The Locust Tree in Flower," this poem focusses none the less purely upon the objects it contains and considers; here, too, the objects are known as the manifestations of their selected qualities. Yet the very qualities that create the men's uniqueness, their distinctive attraction for the poet, are what make them in effect the representatives of all that is best in the

world—its purity and its vitality. The poem works because
it only *presents* the pieces until the reader has established
in his own mind the point of connection that the final
formal simile only reinforces.

The paring down is equally to be found in such a poem
as "Picture of a Nude in a Machine Shop," a typical
Williams' image of the *modernness* of the mechanical,
the technological, and of its vices and virtues. Fuller, less
pared down than either of the previous poems, this is still
a quite bare, spare poem; it relies entirely upon implication for the communication of its "meaning." It is one
complex metaphor in which the equivalences are often
not stated and in which the two main terms, beauty and
function, are not mentioned but merely adumbrated
through the relative values of purity and impurity. If, like
"The RR Bums," this is not one of Williams' *best*
poems, it *is* a good poem primarily by virtue of its
compression, its having been stripped to the evocative
essentials.

This effectiveness of the structural economy in Wil
liams' method does not constitute a claim either for the
inevitability of poetry's ultimate development into such
forms or for the method's superiority over older, more
"conventional" forms. But the utter, stark compression of
this elliptical verse, its strangled, hesitant appearance, its
seeming inarticulateness—the product of all its nervous
energies—the angular, hard, machinelike barrenness, lacking all the appurtenances of traditional "gracefulness"—
these comprise perhaps the essential character of Williams' modernity, his "difference." They declare the latest,
yet still frighteningly unfamiliar, repetition of the poet—
of *man*—hurling himself into his own time. Whether we
like it or not, they constitute the lyric cry of *our* moment
in the world.

It is the supposed inarticulateness of the cry that has in
the past been the focus of much of the derogatory
criticism of Williams. Coming to his poems with values
based in conventional ideas of grammar, his readers have
sought in him something that obviously does not exist—
full, well-articulated sentences in the classic mode. There
is no reason, however, why they should exist here;
Williams would be false to his intention of making an
accurate reflection of his world if he were to attempt a

syntax derived not from modern speech but from past poetic conventions. Rather, he has made his syntactical arrangements as he has made the larger orders of his poems—by the accretion of pieces stripped to the utmost economy. And as a result, he employs neither sentences nor punctuation in the manner of prose. He remarks about his method in a short poem, "The End of the Parade":

> *The sentence undulates*
> *raising no song—*
> *It is too old, the*
> *words of it are falling*
> *apart. Only percussion*
> *strokes continue*
> *with weakening*
> *emphasis what was once*
> *cadenced melody*
> *full of sweet breath.* [b45]

It is obvious that Williams does not ignore or fail to realize the beauties of the past's language. But it is equally manifest that he sees today's language "falling apart"— into fragments, into divorced elements. The grammar that he regards as stultifying is by definition a statement not of what is being done with words but of what has been done; at best it is a guide to educated (past) speech. At the same time, language expresses in its day-to-day changes the realities most difficult to express. As he wrote in an essay, "Excerpts from a Critical Sketch": "We seek a language which will not be at least a deformation of speech as we know it—but will embody all the advantageous jumps, swiftnesses, colors, movements of the day ——" [c109] Perhaps this linguistic search is no more than another reflection of Williams' underlying belief in the local as the only true expression of the universal.

Throughout Williams' work, therefore, one finds him experimenting with syntactical arrangements to find which will best represent the vitality of his language while at the same time they form new measurements, new sense-structures. Side by side with conventional sentences one finds units that are technically sentence fragments but which communicate fully and efficiently what Williams intends to convey; along with "correct" punctuation one sees large areas virtually—or even entirely—unpunctuated, where the subtleties of meaning ordinarily indicated by punctuation marks are expressed instead by line endings, by the words' placement on the page. In at least one sense, this absence of punctuation is the result of Williams' determination that we must have new means of measurement for our poetry; for punctuation is neither more nor less than the traditional means of marking off the units of sense and their relationships, and only by ridding the poem of the established means of measurement can the poet make it adaptable to the new.

The concern over the breakdown of language that is at the intellectual center of *Paterson* is thus Williams' constant concern both with the meanings of words and with their syntactical arrangements, not only in prose, for everyday communications, but especially in the poem. In conversation or writing that is not art, the structural unit, the sentence, should end when the idea is concluded, since the sentence as such is purely a matter of prose mechanics, its business being to carry and transmit intellectual concepts and essentially denotative reports— even of emotions—clearly and accurately. The business of the poem, however, is to feed and stimulate the imagination. If, like Williams, one considers the poem a machine made of words, it is the configuration of the whole machine, the arrangement of its parts, the ways in which they function, that achieves the feeding and stimulation. Yet within each part, in order that some fundamental, if relatively crude, communication be made immediately available, there is always a tendency toward prose at the surface level—the level where the primary denotations and connotations of intellectual and emotional "meanings" are conveyed. The poem, then, accepts its prose materials only insofar as it must use them at the most basic point, the transmission each moment of a sort of foundation of concepts. Over and above this is the transfiguring structure of the imagination—the poem itself, as distinct from its linguistic materials. And so Williams seems to feel it unnecessary in the poem always to construct formally conventional sentences, because grammar is a matter of prose structure rather than of poetic. In fact, the bit of conventional prose syntax used cannot in Williams' method extend past the limit of the moment's piece of (prosaic) actuality to be communicated.

Whether his reasoning about the values of "correct" grammar is good or bad, two things are obvious: first, it is this reasoning that causes the apparent grammatical aberrations in his poems; second, whatever the applicability of his method to prose, his series of sentence fragments and run-on clauses are often exceptionally effective in the poem. The logical conclusion to Williams' idea is, of course, for the poem to divorce itself completely from prose and to use words in a way peculiar to poetry—in the fashion, for instance, of Mallarmé—just as the abstract expressionist painters dispense with *all* representational communication of things in their paintings; but this would mean equally a divorce from the actual world we live in, which would be for Williams an unthinkable act. He realizes that there must be a residue of impurity in every art form—especially in one that communicates at all intellectually, with words. The problem is how to use that impurity profitably.

Williams' task has thus been to invent some means by which he might marry the prose unit to the poetic, make them congruent, and thereby mutually reinforcing rather than mutually destructive. In the twenties he had already ceased to use the sentence as the basic unit of communication, but he seems to have found the uncapitalized, for the most part unpunctuated, run-on statement too unclear: too often entirely ambiguous and too hard to follow for even an immediate emotional comprehension of the poem. With no divisions but the line divisions and the "stanzas"—that is, the blocks of image-complexes—the poem became too much one solid mass; it ceased to have (or to have in sufficient clarity) an arrangement of parts, a formal configuration which he believed a major portion of the poem's "meaning." This was not a matter of making a perceptibly conventional beginning, middle, and end; it was a question of producing a clear indication that like the physical world, the world of his poem was a complex of distinct parts performing, in the poem's structure, their functions in making up the whole.

His first attempt at a solution to the problem was to use capital letters to indicate the beginning of each new sense-unit—whether a complete image or not—and to arrange

the words so that the unit might begin at the beginning of
a line and end at the end of a line. For example, in
"Winter" Williams begins

> *Now the snow*
> *lies on the ground*
> *and more snow*
> *is descending upon it—*
> *Patches of red dirt*
> *hold together*
> *the old*
> *snow patches*
>
> *This is winter—* [a89]

The absence of periods and the use of dashes to mark the
ends of the units does give the reader a feeling of
continuation to come, and Williams went on to use this
technique where he wished to avoid the final bump at the
end of an image, where he wished to express the fundamental oneness of things. In poems such as "Impromptu:
The Suckers," each stanza ends with a dash and the next
begins with a capital; each is a complete unit, but visually
an obvious part of the whole. Only the last stanza closes
with a period, a formal signification of interruption and
ending.

In the method of the poems represented by "Late for
Summer Weather," this use of capitals to indicate the
beginning of a new unit is extended to the indication of
each important term.

> *He has on*
> *an old light grey fedora*
> *She a black beret*
>
> *He a dirty sweater*
> *She an old blue coat*
> *that fits her tight*
>
> *Grey flapping pants*
> *Red skirt and*
> *broken down black pumps*
>
> *Fat Lost Ambling*
> *nowhere through*
> *the upper town they kick*

> *their way through*
> *heaps of*
> *fallen maple leaves*
>
> *still green—and*
> *crisp as dollar bills*
> *Nothing to do. Hot cha!* [a100]

This method is undoubtedly an aid to reading, but it is not an improvement upon conventional punctuation, and Williams discarded the technique after a while in favor of asymmetrically broken lines, lines containing one idea-unit each and set apart on the page. But at this time he was attempting to use some sort of symmetrical stanza—here three lines—with a continuity of language that would indicate the limits of his sense-units while it brought the artificial units, the stanzas, together.

In another poem of the period, "Proletarian Portrait," Williams employs an interesting two-line stanza consisting of one long line and one short which between them make up a unit of idea, an image.

> *A big young bareheaded woman*
> *in an apron*
>
> *Her hair slicked back standing*
> *on the street*
>
> *One stockinged foot toeing*
> *the sidewalk*
>
> *Her shoe in her hand. Looking*
> *intently into it*
>
> *She pulls out the paper insole*
> *to find the nail*
>
> *That has been hurting her* [a101]

Here, in addition to the stanza demarcations, Williams uses both capitalization and line separations to indicate the beginnings and ends of his fragments. Each second line is a qualification of the first, giving information about the how, what, or where of the first statement. Thus, though the first six and a fraction lines, which constitute a sentence fragment, are concluded with a period to indicate that they form one aspect of the view, the remaining image beginning with the capitalized "Looking" is joined to them within a first line because the visual focus of the poem is the shoe, about which everything falls into place: the young woman's act of looking is as closely connected to the shoe as her implicit act of holding it. The poem's lone period serves to show that there are two quite distinct elements, an effect and its cause, while the more purely poetic arrangement of line and stanza illustrate the elements' indissoluble connection.

Among them, these three poems contain the basis of Williams' practice in fitting syntax to the requirements of poetic form. Because they are not brilliant poems, because, that is, they lack the intellectual and emotional penetration of Williams' best work, they are excellent illustrations of his way of making a structure. Their method is typical, true, and not obscured by unique qualities of vision that would overshadow the mechanics of structure: in a sense, these poems are all structure, their values, like their defects, deriving from Williams having *made* them so well out of so little. As he went on, Williams refined some of the elements of his method, but it remained fundamentally unchanged. Even in the complexity of *Paterson* he employs conventional punctuation in his verse only where there is a need for immediate clarity of the prose materials, where, in effect, the verse is not completely *made*; the most highly charged portions, the most purely *poem*, rely most upon capitalization, line, and stanzaic unit for the measurement and delineation of their parts:

> *They begin!*
> *The perfections are sharpened*
> *The flower spreads its colored petals*
> *wide in the sun*
> *but the tongue of the bee*
> *misses them*
> *They sink back into the loam*
> *crying out*
> *—you may call it a cry*
> *that creeps over them, a shiver*
> *as they wilt and disappear:*
> *Marriage come to have a shuddering*
> *implication*

> *Crying out*
> *or take a lesser satisfaction:*
> *a few go*
> *to the Coast without gain—*
> *The language is missing them*
> *they die also*
> *incommunicado.*
>
> *The language, the language*
> *fails them*
> *They do not know the words*
> *or have not*
> *the courage to use them   .*
> *—girls from*
> *families that have decayed and*
> *taken to the hills: no words.*
> *They may look at the torrent in*
> *their minds*
> *and it is foreign to them.   .*
>
> *They turn their backs*
> *and grow faint—but recover!*
> *Life is sweet*
> *they say: the language!*
> *—the language*
> *is divorced from their minds,*
> *the language   .   .   the language!* [e20–21]

In seeking to revitalize a language that fails not only the poet but all the people of his time, in searching for new means of measurement, a way to reunify word and thing, language and poem, by creating a new congruence of prose element and poetic line, Williams also had to find a new metric, some new means of measuring not only the sense of his line but its sound. The old methods, he saw, were useless. They were, to begin with, measurements of a language his world did not speak, of an old-world English rather than a new-world American; furthermore, they were too closely associated with poetic structures from the past, the structures that he wished to replace. Or, to use Williams' own words:

No verse can be free, it must be governed by some measure, but not by the old measure. There Whitman was right but there, at the same time, his leadership failed him. The time was not ready for it. We have to return to some measure but a measure consonant with our time and not a mode so rotten that it stinks. [c339]

And at another time:

> We begin to pick up what so far is little more than a
> feeling . . . that something is taking place in the accepted
> prosody or ought to be taking place. . . . It is similar to
> what must have been the early feelings of Einstein toward
> the laws of Isaac Newton in physics. Thus from being
> fixed, our prosodic values should rightly be seen as only
> relatively true. Einstein had the speed of light as a constant
> —his only constant—What have we? Perhaps our concept
> of musical time. I think so. But don't let us close down on
> that either at least for the moment. [c286]

The discoveries that would lead him to these new laws
of prosody must, of course, come from speech, from
American speech as distinct from English speech, from
what he hears about him rather than from what he reads,
even though his books may be American classics. That the
contemporary language has been in part formed by these
classics is certain; but *their* language is not what we hear,
not what we use, just as we do not use English. This is
important to his conception of the role of the poem's
metric. As he remarked in a letter, once,

> . . . English connotes an historical background from
> which its prosody is derived, which can never be *real* for us.
> It is basic for us to know that the English prosody we
> imitate as a matter of course is not determined by the mere
> facts of the mechanical syllabic sequences but an accretion
> through the ages from English history and character. And
> that these are NOT *our* character. [d269]

To some students of modern American poetry it may
seem redundant to point out Williams' attitude toward
metric, but the fact remains that most readers of his
poems do not know quite how to read them. They search
for some scheme, some mechanical standard of rhythmic
configuration, that will scan, even if ever so loosely.
Especially if they have seen (or heard) any of Williams'
pleas for measure, they are convinced that he must be
working with some notion of a regular, absolute accentual-
syllabic measurement, and they attempt to impose such a
standard in order to make the poems "work out." Failing
this, they tend to give up completely and read it almost as
prose. Yet what Randall Jarrell says in his introduction
to the *Selected Poems* is true: "You've never heard a
Williams poem until you've heard him read it; the listener
realizes with astonished joy that he is hearing a method of

reading poetry that is both excellent and completely unlike anything he has ever heard before." The method of his reading—and of his writing as a transcription of what he hears—is to make a sort of intoned speech interrupted by pauses of varying length; the measure relies less upon the beat of heavily inflected syllables than upon the subtler changes of pace from one series of sounds to another.

The problem for the reader is how he shall recognize the shifts in pace and accentuation; and it is a real one. For all of Williams' idea of an American speech, the fact remains that it is not *one* speech but many, especially where pronunciation and inflection are concerned. Williams writes as he hears and speaks, which is often a way different from his readers' way. And for this reason, unfortunately, there is no sure way of knowing *exactly* how to read a Williams poem. All the reader can do is trust his own ear and his own sense of time; if he considers at all Williams' structural methods—that is, if he tries to see the units of sense that Williams establishes—and adapts the speed and emphases of his speech to the sense of the poem's elements, his reading will approximate Williams' intent. This is not so far from the reading of conventional verse as it seems: one may read, say, iambic pentameter as a succession of precisely regular accentuations, but he will not be reading *a poem*; the poem exists only when he modifies that theoretical symmetry into a more subtle arrangement of speeds and emphases determined by his sense of what is happening in the poem. The difference between the conventional metric and Williams' lies in the fact that for Williams, as for so many of the modern poets,

the stated syllables, as in the best of present-day free verse, have become entirely divorced from the beat, that is the measure. The musical pace proceeds without them.

Therefore the measure, that is to say, the count, having got rid of the words, which held it down, is returned to the *music*. [d326]

Thus:

It's all in
the sound. A song.
Seldom a song. It should

be a song—made of
particulars, wasps,
a gentian—something
immediate, open

scissors, a lady's
eyes—waking
centrifugal, centripetal [b33]

Up to the time of writing *Paterson*, therefore, Williams worked with a metric that was not actually in being but in the process of becoming. In part this accounts for the variety of his verse structures: not having come to a clear idea of *how* to get away from the old metric, he relied upon what sounded "right" to him, what sounded like speech and yet somehow approached the qualities of a song. But with the work on *Paterson* he began to find a relatively stable metrical mode, based upon what he termed "the variable foot." In a letter to Louis Martz, however, he admitted that the excess of his own feelings had made him look for "too big, too spectacular a divergence from the old The 'new measure' is much more particular, much more related to the remote past than I, for one, believed." [d299] The variable foot was an accentuation, not of a syllable, but of a musical (time) period denoted by being written as a line-fragment. Each fragment is, therefore, one foot, variable in that it may contain almost any number of words, or syllables, but constant in its time duration. Divided into three "feet," each "line" becomes a unit in a formal symmetry.

Williams laid out his method in a letter to Richard Eberhart.

    (1) the smell of the heat is boxwood
          (2) when rousing us
               (3) a movement of the air
    (4) stirs our thoughts
          (5) that had no life in them
               (6) to a life, a life in which

(or)

    (1) Mother of God! Our Lady!
          (2) the heart
               (3) is an unruly master:
    (4) Forgive us our sins
          (5) as we
               (6) forgive

(7) those who have sinned against

Count a single beat to each numeral. You may not agree with my ear, but that is the way I count the line. [d326–27]

In effect, what Williams is saying is that because our American idiom tends (at least as he hears it) to slur sounds into a common stress level except where syntax or idea demands emphasis, the poem should (can, must) get away from the usual quantitative measurement and employ a qualitative. That is, since we do not actually distinguish syllables sufficiently by inherent stress, the poet must look at the basic units of statement and measure the sense-stresses, thereby forming a line with their rhythmical beats. And if the poem thus formed is well enough *made*, the three-part line will establish a regularity for the ear without doing violence to the speech that gives it its vitality, while at the same time it will reflect truly the movement of the poet's mind.

Whether the metric based upon the variable foot is in truth the product, as Williams thinks it is, of the historical development of the American language one might argue on various grounds; whether it is the *only* true product is more questionable still. But for Williams it does offer a solution to his problem of measure—*at times*. In the section of *Paterson* (II, 3) where it first appears, it strikes one as perfectly appropriate, an accurate reflection of what Williams is saying and clearly an attempt at measurement—though not clearly of the intensity and duration of sounds—by a relatively symmetrical arrangement of visual units

> The descent beckons
>   as the ascent beckoned
>   Memory is a kind
> of accomplishment
>   a sort of renewal
>   even
> an initiation, since the spaces it opens are new
> places
>   inhabited by hordes
>   heretofore unrealized,
> of new kinds—
>   since their movements
>   are towards new objectives
> (even though formerly they were abandoned) [e96]

As easy as this kind of structure may seem, the continuing section is actually exceptionally difficult to put into an effective structure; the poet could too easily lose control of the materials and permit the more attractive words to usurp more of the reader's attention than they deserve. Thus, since Williams' measurement does create an involuntary, even unconscious, variation in the speed of the reader's speech—whether aloud to listeners or silently to oneself, the poem *is* spoken—the rhythm of the passage helps to reveal the reality of the poem's world. And if one comes to the passage with an understanding of Williams' metrical intent, if he tries to read the lines with the sort of relative regularity that Williams hears in them, one finds previously hidden connections, emphases, shadings of meaning revealing themselves.

On the other hand, an indeterminate amount of the structure's effectiveness derives from the form's imitation of the words' sense; the slanting lines do, after all, offer a visual image of the descent with which the statement opens. Whether there is such a thing as a *fallacy of imitative form* is unimportant; here the similarity between form and "content" is definitely productive of increased powers of communication. Furthermore, maintaining his technique of breaking his lines into sense-units, Williams makes each "foot" serve the dual purpose of counting one "beat" and presenting one idea-fragment toward the accretion of the whole. In fact, from the beginning of the second book, "Sunday in the Park," the poem has been working toward this form; comprising, as the Author's Note to *Paterson* tells us, "the modern replicas" of the elemental characters introduced in the first book, this second section begins to re-form the previously established fragmented materials into new arrangements, one of which seems to be this three-foot line. Book Two opens with a hint of it:

> Outside
>   outside myself
>   there is a world,
>   he rumbled, subject to my incursions
>   —a world
>   (to me) at rest,
>   which I approach
>   concretely— [e57]

But the structure reverts at this point to the arrangements of the first book, and several pages pass before Williams uses the three-element line again—and again only for a moment. Thus, after having encountered the brief out-croppings of this structure at various places, when the reader comes upon a relatively large area of it he is disposed to see this new symmetry as a culmination of the coalescing process, the accretion of things and ideas into a mosaic image, and it is this disposition that releases much of the effective value of the new form.

In the next two books after *Paterson*, however, Williams is not always successful with the variable foot and the three-element line. In both *The Desert Music* and *Journey to Love* the technique is fully developed; Williams uses it surely, adroitly, but it is *too* even, *too* symmetrical for the rest of his technique, which (especially in the short poems) has not changed to meet it. There are still the gaps in statement, the brokenness, the leaps from one thing to another. His poems move in relatively even measure, but his mind doesn't. As a result, if the poems are more smoothly textured, more graceful, they are less interesting as the movements of a unique mind, less exciting.

One final aspect of Williams' structural methods deserves discussion, both for its own sake and for the light it throws upon Williams' attitudes generally toward the making of poems. That is his use of prose in *Paterson*. For the most part the prose sections have been misconstrued by Williams' readers, who have seen them as examples of what Stevens called the "anti-poetic." They are many things, but this they are not. Williams himself has pointed out (in a letter to Horace Gregory among other places) that "The truth is that there's an *identity* between prose and verse, not an antithesis." The two form a continuity in that both are *writing*, and the prose serves in part to show that for Williams even poetry is writing and nothing else. In the context of the mosaic image of *Paterson*, the two forms differ, not in kind, but in the degree of their "madeness." As far back as 1932, in fact, Williams remarked in a letter to Kay Boyle intended as a discussion of literature to be published in the magazine *Contact*, "Prose can be a laboratory for metrics. It is lower in the literary scale. But it throws up jewels which may be cleaned and grouped." In terms of the structure of *Paterson*, therefore, the prose *as writing* serves as one more kind of elemental character for which Williams must make a modern counterpart, a crude form that he must refine for the purposes of his verse.

But the prose sections differ from the verse not only in form, but in the textures of their language, in the sorts of materials they contain (a difference in the natures of the subjects and, often, in the historical times of the occurrences), and in their approaches to, or attitudes toward, their subjects. One thus becomes aware of a counterpoint set up between the prose "raw materials" and the verse "end products" in which there exist comparisons and contrasts (often ironic) between past and present, art and life, reality and actuality. The prose presents the "unmade" facts of the poem's life, either the "historical"—the past from which the present has grown—or, in the several letters, the biographical—the discussion of living as distinct from art. In one sense, therefore, the prose is the actuality that Williams is determined not to lose touch with. Eventually, though, a mild irony begins to appear as the modern counterpart of the earlier, historical, act is played off against its antecedent to show a growth in humanity and civilization not as reality, but as appearance only: actuality in the modern counterpart, the seeming development of civilized—and civil—men, differs, it turns out, from the reality of our time, while in the historically earlier acts the two modes of existence are more nearly identical. For instance, having presented in verse modern men's methods of emasculating and finally attempting to destroy the imagination—which cannot be destroyed: "the life will not out of it"—while men maintain the appearance of supporting and preserving it by the means of a library, Williams inserts a prose passage describing how the colonial authorities tortured, killed, and mutilated two Indians "accused [unfairly, it turned out] of killing two or three pigs." The point of each section separately is the nature of authority—whether formal or informal, official or unofficial—and the relationship between convention and nature (reason and the imagination); but the point of the two together, as a complex whole, is the core of reality remaining unchanged within a constantly changing actual world, and the consequent possibility always of difference between what appears and what is.

In the end, then, with the prose in *Paterson* one comes full circle in Williams' ideas about poetic structure, and indeed about the nature and function of the poem in men's lives. For *Paterson* is in some ways autobiographical, not merely in N. F. Paterson's roles as doctor and poet, but in his role as the personification of place. The place is, after all, the physical point of the accumulation and continuance of life, the physical existence of history, *what happens*; as such it is the concrete evidence of the identity between the processes of American-past becoming American-present and actual life becoming art. The relationship of Revolutionary Paterson to modern Paterson is the relationship of prose to verse, as it is the relationship of N. F. Paterson-as-city—"The multiple seed, / packed tight with detail, soured, . . ."— to N. F. Paterson-as-poet (Williams himself). It is *the act of becoming* that is important, the *making:* the prose—heterogeneous, unordered, irrational—and the verse—unified, measured, distinctive.

> *shells and animalcules*
> *generally and so to man,*
>
> *to Paterson.* [e13]

THE MORE one reads Williams the more one realizes both the unity and the constancy of Williams' ideas about how to make a poem. The conceptual bases for his use of words, therefore, are much the same as the bases for his mode of verse structure—that the words must reflect the poet's own time, that the only "bad" words are those that do not drive the poem further ahead, that American and English are two different dialects (or idioms) almost to the point of being two different languages. Further, just as he refuses to find any materials by nature inadmissible to the poem, he find no words unpoetic except the wrong word for the given place. Thus, since he conceives of the poem as an immediate, true reflection of a culture, being a primary product of it, his various understandings of the culture of his America have various direct effects upon what his poems are, and especially upon the poems' language. For the changing culture of a place makes itself known most immediately in language; the kinds of words commonly used or made taboo, the ways in which words are put together, the variations from the older idiom (the "norm"), these are the agencies by which any new culture (which may be only a transformation of the old) first indicates its essential nature. The new language represents not only the obvious physical things, such as the airplane, or the automobile, or the movies, but the texture of life at the given point in time and place—the attitudes, the feelings, the wishes, the fears of its speakers. And if the poem is to be an imaginative replica of the reality of the poet's world, therefore, that reality must suffuse and direct not only the larger structural arrangements of ideas, sense-units, complex images, whole lines, but the poem's minutenesses of texture, its individual words and phrases, its very sounds.

Thus, Williams' insistence upon what he terms "the American idiom." For Williams it is not enough to say, with Pound, that no good poetry was ever written in a manner twenty years old; also it was never written, it cannot be written, in a language only *like* the language of the place of its intellectual and emotional source. It cannot be written in English, that is, if its cultural matrix is America. This seems by now a self-evident assertion (though more often preached than practiced), but in the early 1900's, when the leaders of intellectual fashion looked to the parent culture as *the* paradigm of excellence, it was a statement that had to be made not only clearly but often. Furthermore, with the accelerating change of the time creating a seeming disjuncture from the past, the shifts both of focus (for the poem, to new materials) and of language (to a new idiom) created difficulties for the poet as well as for the reader and all too often caused a fundamental misunderstanding of Williams' intent.

The outcome of such difficulties and misunderstanding is perhaps best characterized by Stevens' remark about Williams' use of the "anti-poetic." For the term applies not only to the objects and ideas in Williams' poems; surely it must apply most immediately to their language, to their "plain," their "homely" words. Yet clearly there is no such thing as an intrinsically anti-poetic word—unless one assumes that poetry is a convention with clearly delineated and eternally fixed limitations set upon its vocabulary and syntax, so that everything outside that convention is by definition not merely nonpoetic but opposed to the poetic, even destructive to it. That is, one might conceive of prose (or the prosaic) as *ipso facto* anti-poetic because prose denies the validity of form. And in a sense, of course, this sort of antithesis is at the core of Stevens' notion of a "purified" mandarin language for the new poetry. But if in the ideal world of theory this conception is laudable, in the actual realm of poetry as written, like so many other dreams it is impossible nonsense. What the "anti-poetic" was, simply, was the expression of a new world of actuality that could no more be expressed in traditional terms. It was the use of language that reflected not an ideal Poetry (since Poetry does not exist as a useful object in the experience of men; only *poems* do), but the world of things in their constant physical and conceptual change. And in this sense all truly good poems start by being anti-poetic in the very fact of their difference from one or another of the old conventions, in their move into their own moment that they may more nearly express its culture—for examples, the works of Dante, Chaucer, Shakespeare, Wordsworth, all once condemned in part or in whole for being anti-poetic!

One of the major difficulties in Williams' poems is, therefore, the masculine, harsh, at times almost brutal, directness of his language. In considering the things, the ideas, the emotions, the tempo of his world, showing the reader its frequent beauties-in-ugliness, Williams can use only the language available to him as he lives in that world. Yet with the death of conventions, the disjuncture of the present from the poetic past, and with the separation of science from the arts in his technology-ridden time, he finds no common language for men: "divorce" afflicts the poet here, too, "the / language stutters." So, as well as being the maker of poems, he must be the artificer of a language:

> To make a start,
> out of particulars
> and make them general, rolling
> up the sum, by defective means— [e11]

The divorce of word from thing, language from men, forces him to try to forge a "new" language stripped of the old, dead associations and thereby refreshed so as to be capable of precise meanings, precise understandings. It has to be *the* means of immediate contact between men; it will be useful because it will be alive, more truly representative of specific objects than the connotation-encrusted language of conventional poems and thus a more accurate transmitter of Williams' vision. In its directness, its denotativeness, its unconventional precision, it can stimulate the imagination into new, truer modes of thought.

As he has asserted so often, therefore, Williams is not

at the culmination of a tradition, but at its beginning; he is doing the difficult foundation work for the structures of a later "period of mastery." But difficult or no, this transformation of the crude forms of speech into a poetic vehicle is what he has attempted; it is the burden not merely of *Paterson*, but of all his work, and it is thus perhaps a prime cause for so many of his poems appearing only fragments from a larger fabric. In a sense they are just that: hunks of language broken from the common vein and refined, remade, but often not solidly and wholly *poems*. In the compass of *Paterson* there is a continuity of development that successfully fuses the crude (old) words with precise, refined (new) meanings; but the restricted scope of the short poems causes one to feel often that they are written in a language at once familiar and strange—a language with words that look and sound like the words one knows, but the meanings of which are somehow different from what one expected. Reading Williams one feels like an American Alice in a Wonderland where everything is more real than reality but the words don't mean what they're supposed to.

This problem of the transformation of the language is one of the difficulties that finds an answer in Williams' working solution of "no ideas but in things." In the cryptic passage that serves as a sort of epigraph immediately before the preface to *Paterson*, Williams speaks of "in distinctive terms; by multiplication a reduction to one" and "a dispersal and a metamorphosis." In one of their various applications to the subjects in the poem the statements indicate his intention to form a series of new abstractions and generalizations by the synthesis of new (old) poetic (prosaic) details in such fashion that when at the last Williams (or anyone) uses an abstract general term—say, for example, goodness—called up are the new associations with all the chosen specific, concrete details— the good *things* and *acts*—that he has presented as the components, the stimuli, of his poem's world. The fundamental step in the process, therefore, is the identification of concrete thing with idea in a new relationship, the representation of a concept by something denotatively stable, something physical, examinable, and in one imaginative way or another *naturally* related to the idea.

It is for these reasons that just as in the structure of the verse (as artifice), so in the language of the poems Williams takes as his basic unit the image. The image as such permits him to refresh the language by renewing the relationship of word to thing. The process must be imaginative rather than rational, for as the word indicates, the image is the basic unit of the imagination. By the use of materials that are raw, unrefined, materials that are (relatively) in the form in which we are accustomed to experiencing them as actuality, the relationship of word to represented thing, as well as word to word and thing to thing (idea to idea), can be indicated by the poem's structure—implied rather than stated. Thus, a poem by Williams uses fewer similes than conventional poetry does, because simile is a *statement* of relationship. Furthermore, such a relationship assumes set, conventional values for the words it employs; in fact, *only* with such values can a simile be effective. Williams himself has said often that he wants to rid the poem of simile, for mere similarity implies difference that is minimized, or ignored entirely, for the sake of supporting partial likeness, while he wishes to display identity *only* within a maintained individuality.

If the "primitive" language that Williams must use does not often employ simile, then, it can support metaphor, but not always in conventional forms. What makes metaphor useful for Williams is the unexpectedness of the revealed identification within the individuality; this quality is what he wishes to achieve in the renewal of the language. But the conventional A is B form is not always possible where denotatively either A or B, or both, may be insufficently clear and precise as *things*. That is, one or more of the *words* may carry extraneous conventionalized associations and may require isolation in an image to renew its particularity. Williams' solution to this dilemma is a sort of implied metaphor, an indirection very like the indirections of the larger verse structures, in which one term of the metaphor is omitted and must be inferred by the reader: in effect, "is B" or, more grammatically, "B is."

Occasionally, Williams gives the reader the missing term in the title; more often, however, he gives an indication of the direction of his thought in the poem itself. Sometimes he does this by a word or a phrase that turns the reader from the literal meaning to the extended meaning simply by making him aware of that general area of existence. For instance:

Sometimes It Turns Dry and the Leaves Fall before They Are Beautiful

This crystal sphere
upon whose edge I drive
turns brilliantly—
The level river shines!

My love! My love!
how sadly do we thrive:
thistle-caps and
sumac or a tree whose

sharpened leaves
perfect as they are
look no farther than—
into the grass. [b54]

It is true that the title here gives the poem an added subtlety; it is in effect a comment upon the matter of the poem itself. But the indication that the poem is not concerned only with the world of trees and flowers comes from the direct address of the poet to his love. Because of the involvement of people the whole poem becomes a metaphor identifying the natural with the human. Obviously, the purely literal level of trees and flowers is not the concern of the poem; and while the *idea* of the identity may be well worn with use, this real concern of the poem —the brevity of life and the impossibility of success here in one's sole existence—is made valid by the precision and truth of the detail.

Most often, of course, Williams uses the juxtaposition of images to establish a sort of metaphor. Use of the image as such permits him to stimulate and direct the imagination, and his placing of images side by side without stating their relationship insures the autonomy of each, and therefore the purity and propriety of its literal meaning, as, for example, in the section of "To All Gentleness" beginning with "Copernicus, / Shostako-witch. Is it the occasion / or the man? . . ." and concluding ". . . Bombs away / and the packed word descends— and / rightly so. / The arrow! The arrow!" [b27–28] By clearing his terms of possible extraneous associations Williams creates the new connections between what *he* regards as the real nature of violence and the real nature of gentleness, both finally aspects of art, inherent qualities of the word. The associations are here carefully established for the reader, culminating in the arrow as representative of all directed things, themselves symbolized by the bomb-word identity. Thus, Williams accomplishes two things at once: in the larger units of verse structure he presents the complex relationships of gentleness and violence as abstract generalizations, their opposition-and-sameness, and in the word-to-word structures of his language he establishes newly specific "meanings" for the words themselves.

To assume a real and definable distinction between word-as-word and word-as-idea is, as remarked previously, an artifice at the same time fallacious and necessary, both qualities nowhere more clearly discernible than in the last piece of a poem, where Williams' intent is to pack the word with meaning not only more complex but more precise than it would have in ordinary usage, to free it to derive new senses and new clarity from its context. If the important words here are all as purely denotative as Williams can make them, this denotativeness is the fundamental quality of *all* Williams' work. For though obviously the word is denotatively never the reality itself, but only a signification of that reality—a symbol—the question must always arise as to how the poet uses that symbol and where he gets it; does he employ it *merely* as symbol, saying, in effect, "In the beginning is the word; later I shall give it meaning"; or does he attempt to find that word which will unobtrusively call up the reality that he seeks to signify? That is, is the word used arbitrarily, or merely conventionally, or is it inherently connected somehow with the thing (idea)?

Williams believes that the poet must "refresh" words by stripping away their conventional connotations and redirecting the reader's attention away from the haze of the purely ideational and back to the reality in and of the things represented, which have in themselves sufficient associational values. In an essay rebuking Rebecca West for demeaning James Joyce, Williams once said something of the sort:

Joyce maims words. Why? Because meanings have been dulled, then lost, then perverted by their connotations (which have grown over them) until their effect on the mind is no longer what it was when they were fresh, but grows rotten as *poi*—though we may get to like *poi*.

Meanings are perverted by time and chance—but kept perverted by academic observance and intention. At worst they are inactive and get only the static value of anything, which retains its shape but is dead. All words, all sense of being gone out of them. Or trained into them by the dull of the deadly minded. Joyce is restoring them.

. . . .

Joyce has not changed the words beyond recognition. They remain to a quick eye the same. But many of the stultifying associations of the brutalized mind (brutalized by modern futility) have been lost in his process.

The words are freed to be understood again in an original, a fresh, delightful sense.

Lucid they do become. Plain, as they have not been for a lifetime, we see them. [c89–90]

Williams' attitude toward language is thus consistent with his various other conceptions of the nature of the life of the mind. It is his belief that ideas change, associations change, attitudes change—only things in themselves remain (or *can* remain) unchanged. Thus, the use of the denotative word and the careful establishment of modern associations. And thus, too, Williams' choice of "non-poetic" words for their very unconventionality as the language of the poem, their freshness, their purity.

Williams has, in effect, always used symbols; the weakness of some of his late work—from perhaps 1950 on and especially in *The Desert Music*—is due not to a sudden interest in symbols, but to the symbols' being arbitrary rather than organic parts of the wholes. As a matter of fact, even in his Imagist poems, where the-thing-itself is theoretically all important, Williams invested his phenomena—human as well as natural and mechanical—with an implication of their symbolizing, their representing, areas of larger importance. As he developed, his investing of things with extra-objective reference remained the use of *what was there*: the thing is important not because it stands for another, but because it is a typical example of a whole class that includes it and others, and for all of which it becomes an epitome. Each—the specific thing

written about and the thing(s) implied—is important in
its own right; each has its own propriety of existence. And
for Williams, as for all moral poets, propriety in this true
sense is a terribly important matter. But in the late poems
there is often a shift of attention from the thing stated,
which loses its propriety of existence and becomes a falsity
(a decoration) in the real world of the poem, to the thing
implied, which is perhaps too vague, perhaps too complex
intellectually for direct expression by typification in some
physical object. Surface reality is lost, and so the poetry
dies.

Now, this is a problem not merely of the poems' objects
but of the relationship between word and object and thus
of the kinds of words Williams chooses to use. Clearly the
archetypal object will be best represented by the word
that carries with it the fewest extraneous connotations. To
call a ship a ship is to denote the nature and function of
the object; to call it a clipper, or a liner, or a tub, is to
indicate certain conventional attitudes not only toward
the object, but toward comfort, speed, cleanliness, past *vs.*
present, and a horde of other concepts. Equally clearly,
though, no word is *entirely* free from connotations; even
the most modern terms have, if nothing else, the implication of modernity, of being restrictively located in time
and place. Since it is Williams' desire to make his poems
specific in just that way, however, whenever there is the
choice of new word or old word, Williams is inclined to
use the new. Thus in diction as well as in syntax Williams
moves always toward language as it is spoken, its directness, its quickness, its clarity, its purity of meaning
magnified in the artifice of the poem.

Such a poem as the title section of "Spring and All"
shows Williams' language at its best.

> *By the road to the contagious hospital*
> *under the surge of the blue*
> *mottled clouds driven from the*
> *northeast—a cold wind. Beyond, the*
> *waste of broad, muddy fields*
> *brown with dried weeds, standing and fallen*
>
> *patches of standing water*
> *the scattering of tall trees*

All along the road the reddish
purplish, forked, upstanding, twiggy
stuff of bushes and small trees
with dead, brown leaves under then
leafless vines—

Lifeless in appearance, sluggish
dazed spring approaches—

They enter the new world naked,
cold, uncertain of all
save that they enter. All about them
the cold, familiar wind—

Now the grass, tomorrow
the stiff curl of wildcarrot leaf
One by one objects are defined—
It quickens: clarity, outline of leaf

But now the stark dignity of
entrance—Still, the profound change
has come upon them: rooted, they
grip down and begin to awaken [a241–42]

Here is the precision that Pound asked for, "that explicit rendering, be it of external nature or of emotion." Here Williams relies upon common words for his (un)-common scene—the exact, primarily denotative words that most accurately present (which is to say, represent) the physical existence of the poem's world. The manner of presentation is (though Williams would object to the term) scientific, clinical; the poet's intent is communicated primarily not by the words themselves but, through them, by the objects signified and their typical qualities.

Along with Williams' determination to use the common words one finds Williams' desire to take over into the poem both the syntax and the terminology of slang. Attracted by its vitality and its expressive rapidity, in addition to its newness, he tries often to incorporate it as is in his poems—to capture its moment and hold it alive. For instance, in "At the Bar":

Hi, open up a dozen.

Wha'cha tryin' ta do—
charge ya batteries?

Make it two.

Easy girl!
You'll blow a fuse if
ya keep that up. [a431]

Even if one grants Williams his conclusion that all modes of language are equally acceptable to the poem, one can object to this poem as one objects to other too-short poems of Williams': that although this is a fragment of Williams' world it is *too much* a fragment, it is too little made into a *significant* replica of that world. The slanginess is cut off from all that forms it and all that it represents. Here Williams has violated his own principle of wholeness and has permitted himself to be seduced by the mere differentness, the (for the poem) exotic immediacy, of slang and only used it for its own sake. Interestingly, though, when he takes this fragment later and imbeds it in *Paterson* as one of the many minutiae of the larger poem, it works with reasonable success as a bit of raw material for the poem's process of accretion and refinement. There its crude energy, its primitiveness, reveals in one more way the ironic development of present from past and the inarticulateness of modern men, divorced from their own language.

Perhaps more successful because presented ironically rather than seriously is "Graph for Action," though here too the poem is too slight to come to much more than an amusing finger exercise.

Don't say "humbly."
"Respectfully," yes
but not "humbly."

And the Committee
both farted
and that settled it. [a431]

Like so many of the prose writers of his time, Williams is attracted to the no-nonsense words for bodily functions. In an attempt to startle the reader into a realization of the inherent goodness and purity of the physical, Williams uses material that demands equal indelicacy of language — for example, in "Turkey in the Straw":

I'll put this in my diary:

On my 65th birthday
I kissed her while she pissed

(Your thighs are apple trees
whose blossoms touch the sky!)

On my 65th birthday
I tussled her breasts.
She didn't even turn away
*   but smiled!*

It's your 65th birthday!

(I kissed her while she pissed) [b204]

The defect of this latter poem lies not in its subject, but in the objects and words employed for the communication of the ideas. The continuation of love into old age and man's continuing delight in the physical as the manifestation of his love are important. Yet the poem is ineffective; the conflict between the conventional attitudes toward the two actions is only reinforced by the word "pissed" instead of coming to the resolution that Williams sees in the oneness of all natural physicality. Supporting the active harshness of "pissed" by its contrast is the parenthetical stanza, quoted from one of Williams' early poems, which in its youthfully imaginative escape from reality forms the romantic center which Williams shows he has not left even now in a world of aging, bare actuality. But the *world* of actuality is usurped here by the mere *word* of actuality, and in our undue attention to the one word we lose sight of what it represents. Nor would any other word serve better; a weaker term would be no more than a euphemism, an admission of concern about the propriety of the whole poem and consequently its defeat. "Pissed" is the only word possible, but because it is not *purely* denotative, because it has not been "renewed," because it calls up the associations of social crudity rather than of mere acceptance of physicality, it is the wrong word.

If there is one fundamental shortcoming of Williams' use of "anti-poetic" words, therefore, it lies in their very strength. Such language can reflect—or illuminate—only a portion of the poet's subject, or vision, and in some areas of the poem only one part of the immediate fragment of subject, one of the tendencies in men's nature (as here regarding sex). But the vitality of these words is often such that they appear (perhaps even to the poet himself) to comprise a statement of the whole subject; their unusualness in their context calls undue attention to them and thereby draws attention away from the justly equal demands of the other material.

In his better work Williams seems to recognize the dangers of imbalance and the necessity for a variety of expression. For the most part he maintains a delicately articulated alternation of informal speech and artificial literary construction that becomes in the end an enveloping structure of precisely arranged syntax that limits and directs the energies of the colloquial that is straining to expand and break out of the poetic restrictions. In such a poem as "A Vision of Labor: 1931," [b42–43] for example, Williams manages to extend the capacities of the slice of life method by the use of juxtapositions of artificial and colloquial language, each presenting its own kind of image and each, in turn, representing a different part of the world, the poetic (or poet's) imagination and its products as distinct from (connected with) the desensitized world of the pressures of actuality.

The poem starts as direct statement of the poet's thought, his awareness of himself *as poet*, and the language is formally "made," especially in the syntactically unusual placement of "otherwise" and the use of such educated diction as "juxtapositions." From this the poem progresses away from the subjectivity of the poet's thought to the objective world about him, reverting to his subjective world at times through the recollection of Rome and the precise, relatively formal syntactical arrangements in which the recollection is presented. But always the poem moves outward, even the thought of the Forum offering a means of providing greater associational values for the scene, of extending its implications by both the similarities and the differences implicit in the juxtapositions. The language grows more and more purely the language of colloquial speech, therefore, until it reaches its apogee in the poet's own "Geezus. What the hell / kind of water is that to drink?" Linguistically at least, the poet has become an elemental part of the wholly unified scene. And for the remainder of the poem the unity of the

originally disparate elements is held not only in the
shifting back and forth between the world and the poet's
comments on it, but in the consistent (though delicately
varied) colloquial tone of the language.

Such dualities of usage in syntax and diction are
constant in Williams' work, providing him with a means
for freeing the mind by freeing the language. Throughout
his writing he maintains a flexibility of poetic speech that
admits to its realm all modes of locution, from which
variety he attempts to develop an active, accurate replica
of the diversity of his world. Especially in *Paterson* is this
attempt clear; there Williams associates the water of the
river both with the flow of time and with language, the
means of continuity and traffic among men. The river
animates the city and the man, as water and as language,
and connects each with its origins and the reality of its
nature. Thus, after the prose section of history describing
the visit of the Rev. Cumming and Mrs. Cumming to
the Passaic Falls and her fall into them and drowning,
Williams reverts to the theme of the loss of language:

A *false language. A true. A false language pouring—a
language* (*misunderstood*) *pouring* (*misinterpreted*) *without
dignity, without minister, crashing upon a stone ear.* [e24]

The language must be remade, understood anew, the ear
must regain its sensitivity, else all life, all possibility of
human fulfilment, fails. Without the ministry of the poet,
we cannot realize ourselves.

> *The language, the language*
> *fails them*
> *They do not know the words*
> *or have not*
> *the courage to use them.*
> *—girls from*
> *families that have decayed and*
> *taken to the hills: no words.*
> *They may look at the torrent in*
> *their minds*
> *and it is foreign to them.   .* [e20–21]

The problem for Williams, as for so many other poets,
is how to construct the poem so that it *seems* conversational while at the same time it gains from its artifice a
distinction that makes it significant and memorable.

What Williams seeks (in its theoretical perfection) is not
merely a replica of how men do speak, but a paradigm for
an ideal speech to be made from the defective materials at
his (our) disposal.

> *There is no direction. Whither? I*
> *cannot say. I cannot say*
> *more than the how. The how (the howl) only*
> *is at my disposal (proposal): watching—*
> *colder than stone   .*
>
>   *a bud forever green,*
> *tight-curled, upon the pavement, perfect*
> *in juice and substance but divorced, divorced*
> *from its fellows, fallen low—*
>
>   *Divorce is*
> *the sign of knowledge in our time,*
> *divorce! divorce!*
>
>   *with the roar of the river*
> *forever in our ears (arrears)*
> *inducing sleep and silence, the roar*
> *of eternal sleep   .   .   challenging*
> *our waking—*
>
> *—unfledged desire, irresponsible, green,*
> *colder to the hand than stone,*
> *unready—challenging our waking:*
>
> *Two halfgrown girls hailing hallowed Easter,*
> *(an inversion of all out-of-doors) weaving*
> *about themselves, from under*
> *the heavy air, whorls of thick translucencies*
> *poured down, cleaving them away,*
> *shut from the light: bare-*
> *headed, their clear hair dangling—*
>
> *Two—*
>   *disparate among the pouring*
> *waters of their hair in which nothing is*
> *molten—*
>
> *two, bound by an instinct to be the same:*
> *ribbons, cut from a piece,*
> *cerise pink, binding their hair: one—*
> *a willow twig pulled from a low*

leafless bush in full bud in her hand,
(or eels or a moon!)
holds it, the gathered spray,
upright in the air, the pouring air,
strokes the soft fur—

        Ain't they beautiful!

Certainly I am not a robin nor erudite,
no Erasmus nor bird that returns to the same
ground year by year. Or if I am . .
the ground has undergone
a subtle transformation, its identity altered.

Indians!

Why even speak of "I," he dreams, which
interests me almost not at all?

                The theme
is as it may prove: asleep, unrecognized—
all of a piece, alone
in a wind that does not move the others—
in that way: a way to spend
a Sunday afternoon while the green bush
shakes.

.   .   a mass of detail
to interrelate on a new ground, difficulty;
an assonance, a homologue
                  triple piled
pulling the disparate together to clarify
and compress

The river, curling, full—as a bush shakes
and a white crane will fly
and settle later! White, in
the shallows among the blue flowered
pickerel-weed, in summer, summer! if it should
ever come, in the shallow water!

          On the embankment a short,
compact cone (juniper)
that trembles frantically
in the indifferent gale: male—stands
rooted there   .

The thought returns: Why have I not
but for imagined beauty where there is none

or none available, long since
put myself deliberately in the way of death?

> *Stale as a whale's breath: breath!*
Breath!

> *Patch leaped but Mrs. Cumming shrieked*
> *and fell—unseen (though*
> *she had been standing there beside her hus-*
> *band half*
> *an hour or more twenty feet from the edge).*

> *: a body found next spring*
> *frozen in an ice-cake; or a body*
> *fished the next day from the muddy swirl—*

> *both silent, uncommunicative*

> *Only of late, late! begun to know, to*
> *know clearly (as through clear ice) whence*
> *I draw my breath or how to employ it*
> *clearly—if not well:*

> *Clearly!*
> *speaks the red-breast his behest. Clearly!*
> *clearly! [e28–31]*

This is Williams' language at its mature best. In the broad scope of the long poem it attains a unique personality, becomes in its variety fully communicative. Its range extends from the educated diction of "assonance" and "homologue" to the ironically revealing inarticulateness of "Ain't they beautiful" It is a voice speaking, yet it can employ thoroughly unspeechlike locutions, omissions of words (especially subjects), compressions of structure—and thereby gain in clarity.

In a sense the other side of Williams' precision-in-denotativeness achieved by his openness to all levels of word usage is his compression of language, the characteristic strippedness of his poems. Here too one sees the incredible singleness of Williams' purpose, for the use of the denotative image dictates the rooting out of all words that do not add momentum to the poem's drive toward complete activity: every word must have not only mass but energy. Thus, for instance, the grammatical subject once stated, it adds no further impetus to the poem if repeated; rather, it must be made sufficiently strong in the first place to remain in the mind able to couple with later particles of action that accrete around it. By the same token, participial verb forms occur with unusual frequency in Williams' verse. Their use too is understandable in the light of the poem's structural intent: indicating as they do continuing action rather than any specific placement in time, they form a sort of eternal present, a now in which the action is always occurring, demanding an agent, and thereby they form active images of the world in its movement.

Obviously such grammatical incompletenesses are necessary for the implementation of Williams' entire esthetic theory. It is only in the gaps between elements of the poem that the imagination can create its new structures; for Williams to present everything with any sense of finality would be for him to intrude between the objects and the reader and thus to inhibit the reader's realization of the nature of things. Again one comes back to the desired identity between idea and thing—or to Williams' curious metaphorical wish for words to turn from water to stone. For the poem achieves in its language a solidity and a permanence by fixing the fluid words in a structure, by an ordering of the disparate, often shapeless parts.

> *A quatrain? Is that*
> *the end I envision?*
> *Rather the pace*
> *which travel chooses.*
>
> *Female? Rather the end*
> *of giving and receiving*
> *—of love: love surmounted*
> *is the incentive.*
>
> *Hardly. The incentive*
> *is nothing surmounted,*
> *the challenge lying*
>   *elsewhere.*
>
> *No end but among words*
> *looking to the past,*
> *plaintive and unschooled,*
> *wanting a discipline*
>
> *But wanting*
> *more than discipline*

a rock to blow upon
as a mist blows

or rain is driven
against some
headland jutting into
a sea—with small boats

perhaps riding under it
while the men fish
there, words blowing in
taking the shape of stone

.   .   .   .

Past that, past the image:
a voice!
out of the mist
above the waves and

the sound of waves, a
voice   .   speaking! [b171–72]

What makes a discussion of Williams' language most difficult is undoubtedly this dual character of commonness and compression. Unlike Eliot or Pound, whose language is more traditionally "educated" and often exotic, and unlike Stevens, whose diction is more limited, more conventional, and more carefully chosen for nuances of pure sound, Williams offers no definable idiosyncratic vocabulary or style of phrasing to examine as a key to the whole pattern. Least of all does he ever have an elegance of language that one might point to. Elegance is foreign to him and, as he sees it, foreign to America. In this he is, as he has at times conceived of himself, an heir to Whitman and the Whitmanesque democratic ideal. It is easy to see how a poet who regards the nature of America as Williams does would find it imperative, in his attempt to capture the culture of his time and place in poems, to employ a heterogeneous, democratically all-inclusive language. It would be incongruous, and therefore untruthful, to present ditchdiggers or factory workers in terms designed for the drawing room. It would be unrealistic to offer in uncommon language a vision of the world as a common place. For Williams' elegance is clearly a quality of an aristocratic society; it is the product of a static state with established values and is, therefore, antithetical to the purification and perfection of the understanding of a developing, half-formed America.

What Williams does possess is not elegance, then, but strength—an exciting and pleasing directness that in its deceptive conversational tone achieves, at its best, the power of natural simplicity. If his poems often seem flat, they do so because the intellectual and emotional life of modern America is flat, we have not yet forged the language with which to communicate the heightened moments of our lives—even to ourselves. Yet where Williams does manage to find the language capable of being refreshed, he causes it to go past mere elegance to a harmoniousness, a propriety, that draws the reader into the poem's world and satisfies him in its purity. Here the senses are heightened by the cleanliness of the words, by their rapidity—the flash of lightning rather than the long roll of thunder.

NOTES

Citations in the text are to the following books by William
Carlos Williams:

    a. *The Collected Earlier Poems of William Carlos
       Williams* (Norfolk, Conn.: New Directions,
       1951).
    b. *The Collected Later Poems of William Carlos
       Williams* (Norfolk, Conn.: New Directions,
       1950).
    c. *Selected Essays of William Carlos Williams* (New
       York: Random House, 1954).
    d. *The Selected Letters of William Carlos Williams*
       (New York: McDowell, Obolensky, 1957).
    e. *Paterson* (New York: New Directions, 1963).

1 — To Make a Start, Out of Particulars

  1. T. S. Eliot, *Selected Essays* (New York: Harcourt,
Brace & Co., 1932), pp. 124–25.
  2. As I see it, myth is in this sense the expression of a
culture's common-understanding (values) in terms of actions
and attitudes that are in that culture considered typical; but
the specific form (combination) of these (the story) is
unique.
  3. William Carlos Williams, *Spring and All* (N.p.: Contact Publishing Co., 1923), p. 3.
  4. William Carlos Williams, *The Autobiography of William Carlos Williams* (New York: Random House, 1951), p.
241.
  5. Ezra Pound, *ABC of Reading* (Norfolk, Conn.: New
Directions, n.d.), pp. 47–48.
  6. Kenneth Burke, "Heaven's First Law," *The Dial*,
LXXII (February, 1922), 197.

7. *Ibid.*, p. 200.

8. Vivienne Koch, *William Carlos Williams* (Norfolk, Conn.: New Directions, 1950), pp. 37–38.

9. For instance in "The Waste Land," line 260; but the *thing* exists unnamed or in synonym in several other places.

10. Koch, *Williams*, p. 25.

11. I don't mean to imply that this is a *purely* modern split —merely that my scope is the modern, and it exists now (because of wider "literacy") in a perhaps more virulent and more widespread way than in the past.

12. This applies as well to the faddists, like the "Beat Generation," who are merely inarticulate about their "religious profundities."

13. William Carlos Williams, *Collected Poems, 1921–1931*, preface by Wallace Stevens (New York: The Objectivist Press, 1934), p. 2.

14. *Ibid.*, p. 2.

2 – And Make Them General

1. Ezra Pound, *The Literary Essays of Ezra Pound*, ed. with intro. by T. S. Eliot (Norfolk, Conn.: New Directions, 1954), p. 43.

2. *Ibid.*, p. 44.

3. William Carlos Williams, *I Wanted to Write a Poem*, ed. Edith Heal (Boston: Beacon Press, 1958), p. 57.

4. Williams has remarked (e.g., in his *Autobiography*) about Keats having been his early model and influence, but the more one considers Williams' poetry the more one is struck by its similarity to Blake's, not only in their reaction to the mechanical and industrial depersonalization of men, but down to their specific ideas about the need for contact through love, about marriage and sex—even about what a poem should be.

5. William Carlos Williams, *Kora in Hell: Improvisations* (San Francisco: City Lights Books, 1962), pp. 23–24.

6. F. O. Matthiessen, *The Achievement of T. S. Eliot* (New York: Oxford University Press, 1947), p. 63.

7. Vivienne Koch, *William Carlos Williams* (Norfolk, Conn.: New Directions, 1950), p. 57.

8. Pound maintains in his essays that poetry *must not* be didactic. He is thinking, of course, of the hortatory and the moralizing.

9. See pp. 87–89 for a discussion of the poem.

10. Koch, *Williams*, p. 41.

11. Ezra Pound, *The Letters of Ezra Pound*, ed. D. D.

Paige with preface by Mark Van Doren (New York: Harcourt, Brace & Co., 1950), p. 124.

12. This is not merely another way of saying that he is a realist; as a matter of fact, if one uses the accepted definitions of literary realism, he isn't. But then, "realism," like "good" and "evil," usually means whatever the user wishes.

13. William Carlos Williams, *Paterson*, flap of dust jacket for original edition (1949).

14. Just as the artist needs some foundation in group effort, the reader needs the group understanding, the common consciousness, in order to be able not only to accept the rightness of the artist's insights, but even to comprehend them.

3—Rolling Up the Sum

1. Ezra Pound, *ABC of Reading* (Norfolk, Conn.: New Directions, n.d.), pp. 47–48.

BIBLIOGRAPHY

Burke, Kenneth. "Heaven's First Law, *The Dial*, LXXII (February, 1922).

Eliot, T. S. *Selected Essays*. New York: Harcourt, Brace and Co., 1932.

Koch, Vivienne. *William Carlos Williams*. Norfolk, Conn.: New Directions, 1950.

Matthiessen, F. O. *The Achievement of T. S. Eliot*. New York: Oxford University Press, 1947.

Pound, Ezra. *ABC of Reading*. Norfolk, Conn.: New Directions, n.d.

————. *The Letters of Ezra Pound*. Ed. D. D. Paige with preface by Mark Van Doren. New York: Harcourt, Brace and Co., 1950.

————. *The Literary Essays of Ezra Pound*. Ed. with intro. by T. S. Eliot. Norfolk, Conn.: New Directions, 1954.

Williams, William Carlos. *The Autobiography of William Carlos Williams*. New York: Random House, 1951.

————. *The Collected Earlier Poems of William Carlos Williams*. Norfolk, Conn.: New Directions, 1951.

————. *The Collected Later Poems of William Carlos Williams*. Norfolk, Conn.: New Directions, 1950.

————. *Collected Poems 1921–1931*. Preface by Wallace Stevens. New York: The Objectivist Press, 1934.

————. *The Desert Music and Other Poems*. New York: Random House, 1954.

————. *I Wanted to Write a Poem*. Reported and edited by Edith Heal. Boston: Beacon Press, 1958.

————. *Journey to Love*. New York: Random House, 1955.

————. *Kora in Hell*. San Francisco: City Lights Books, 1962.

————. *Paterson*. New York: New Directions, 1963.

————. *Pictures from Brueghel and Other Poems*. New York: New Directions, 1962.

————. *Selected Essays of William Carlos Williams*. New York: Random House, 1954.

————. *The Selected Letters of William Carlos Williams.*
New York: McDowell, Obolensky, 1957.
————. *Spring and All.* N.p.: Contact Publishing Co.,
1923.

INDEX